A PRACTICAL GUIDE TO RESEARCH METHODS

Sixth Edition

Gerhard Lang
George D. Heiss

University Press of America,® Inc.
Lanham • New York • Oxford

Copyright © 1975,1979,1984,1991,1994,1998 by
Gerhard Lang and George D. Heiss

University Press of America,® Inc.
4720 Boston Way
Lanham, Maryland 20706

12 Hid's Copse Rd.
Cummor Hill, Oxford OX2 9JJ

Library of Congress Cataloging-in-Publication Data

Lang, Gerhard.
A practical guide to research methods / Gerhard Lang, George D.
Heiss. —6th ed.
p.   cm.
Includes bibliographical references and index.
l. Research—Methodology. I. Heiss, George D. II. Title.
Q180.55.M4L36   1997   001.4'2—DC21   97-44434 CIP

ISBN 0-7618-0979-1 (cloth: alk. ppr.)
ISBN 0-7618-0980-5 (pbk: alk. ppr.)

IN LOVING MEMORY

of

GEORGE D. HEISS

Friend

Colleague

Educator

Preface

It is no secret that introductory courses in statistics and research are some of the least popular in the academic program and that the typical student approaches them with many uncertainties and anxieties. The authors also believe that students have been short-changed for years by those research and methods textbooks which gave little or no recognition to qualitative research techniques.

This book has been written in an attempt to stimulate interest in and to improve the usefulness of the introductory research course by focusing the material on the needs of the neophyte researcher.

To accomplish this end, this book:

1) uses examples from the writers' own experiences as researchers and teachers, thus making the content more meaningful;
2) employs, for the most part, a conversational tone rather than the usual formal style of writing;
3) presents the content itself in clear and succinct language;
4) integrates practical statistical applications where appropriate;
5) directs the material to all beginning students in research.

The authors believe that all educated persons should have some understanding of the research process. We do not agree that research skills and understanding should only be held by a relatively small group of so-called experts. Even those who claim to see no value in research are affected by it. People in business and the professions are more frequently being asked to either participate in a research project or to accept and use concepts, skills, and materials developed through research. The authors believe that at the very least, one ought to be able to ask informed questions about such research and that the best way to become informed is to get involved in the process.

The first edition of this book emerged after extensive experimentation with preliminary versions of this material in our courses. Subsequent editions incorporated many suggestions offered by our students and colleagues who used this book. In addition, several chapters were updated and new material was added.

Any suggestions and comments are most welcome and should be addressed to Dr. Gerhard Lang at Montclair State University, Upper Montclair, NJ 07043.

The authors are greatly indebted to Dr. Thomas Perera for his contributions to Chapter 4 and to Dr. Mark Weinstein for his worthwhile suggestions.

The manuscript was expertly typed by Snezana Epstein.

Gerhard Lang

George D. Heiss

Table of Contents

#1: Introduction to Research

In this chapter we shall deal with: (1) a conception of what research is all about; (2) different levels of training in and doing research, with special emphasis on this course; and (3) some terms which are used in the research literature.

The Research Process

We believe it is best to understand research by asking three basic questions:
  (a) <u>What</u> is research?
  (b) <u>Why</u> are research methods used?
  (c) <u>How</u> are these research methods used?

Any firs rate dictionary will give you a definition of "research." We are not concerned about a refined definition. Essentially, "research" is a <u>systematic</u> and <u>unbiased</u> way of solving a problem (by answering questions and supporting hypotheses) through generating verifiable data. The hallmark of the researcher is <u>not</u> the sophisticated equipment nor the shiny laboratory, but a way of thinking and tackling a problem. A good researcher is a person who approaches a problem with an open, unbiased mind and solves it in an orderly, systematic manner. Sophisticated hardware and various tools, such as high speed computers, are but the means to solve the problem. They are no substitute for the objective, unbiased mind, and one major objective of a research course is to develop in the student such traits as these which some believe are basic to a scientific attitude. Weakness here sometimes occurs at the highest levels. For example, some years ago a scientist at the famed Memorial Sloan-Kettering Cancer Center was fired because he misrepresented the findings of transplants on mice and rabbits.

The scientific way of solving problems stretches back to Aristotle and in the early 20th century was reformulated by John Dewey and brought into the mainstream of contemporary thought. Dewey's theory of cognition which identifies the basic elements of the inductive-deductive process has been helpful to many, including the scientist, educational researcher, and even the curriculum developer. For example, various problem solving approaches to teaching like the Discovery Method are based on this theory.

Dewey's schema for cognition, which may be familiar to you, follows:[1]

1. Intermediate situation – a puzzling situation
2. Clarification of situation – define the problem
3. Formulation of hypothesis – intelligent guesses or assumptions which attempt to answer the problem
4. Collection, organization and analysis of data – ongoing through all steps
5. Formulation of possible conclusions
6. Verification, rejection or modification – selected a hypothesis by a test of its consequences in specific situations.

While this pattern is a worthwhile formulation to develop understanding of a scientific way of thinking and operating, it is not the only method of applying logic and observation to problem solving. Furthermore, even though all the sciences share the goal and methods of science, because their specific purposes and subjects are different they use the various steps and parts of the system differently. An overly rigid definition and practice of the research process would omit many ways in which researchers go about their tasks.

Why Use Research Methods

Why do we use research methods in solving problems rather than rely on alternatives? Several other ways of developing knowledge exist, such as reliance on authority, on personal experiences, on common sense, and on intuition. Are these options acceptable and dependable? We maintain that none of them are good alternatives to research as a means of problem solving. One authority may be superseded by another authority. Or suppose an authority wields excessive power and asserts a "truth" that is in fact not verifiable, yet oppressive. Personal experience obviously are limited and biased. "Common sense" notions often consist of half truths, hearsay evidence, and downright wishful thinking. Intuition or the apprehension of knowledge by the mind through a sudden insightful grasp, or instructive self-consciousness, or a mystical communication through a religious or some kind of extrasensory experience may be interesting and useful. However, it too has its limitations because of its private nature and difficulty of verification. Really, how does one distinguish the crackpot from the true prophet? While these ways of knowing are useful and can be complementary rather than contradictory, they are not enough.

---

[1] See Dewey (1991)

We suggest that research approaches based on scientific methods are the most reliable way to move from limited, biased perceptions and opinions to fact or tentative truth. Perhaps one of the outstanding characteristics of this type of procedure is its openness to the public test – that is, one's procedures and data are open to the scrutiny of one's colleagues. Thus, when errors are detected, the rest of the system operates to overcome them. No other way of truth-seeking has this characteristic. Because of the self-correcting nature of science, many people regard it as the most powerful way to gain knowledge or objective truth.

How to Use Research Methods

Now let us consider how research methods are used and, sometimes, misused. There are several legitimate, ethical uses of research methods. For instance, researchers are involved with the development of all kinds of products or materials, a safer and more economical car, fire-resistant fabrics, manmade substitutes for diminishing natural raw materials, educational tests and techniques, etc. Research techniques are also appropriately applied in the evaluation of various products, programs, or projects. Some of these evaluations consist of comparison testing of various products as undertaken, for example, by Consumers Union. Other evaluations call for controlled experiments – for example, a study of the effectiveness of artificial blood or a study of the effectiveness of a compensatory reading program. But should research methods be used to justify or legitimize certain products, programs or projects? For instance, should a researcher design a study in such a way that potentially harmful car components will appear to be safe? Or should another researcher evaluate a politically sensitive educational project like sex education with the view of getting positive results? One of our colleagues working for a large urban school system once put it quite well when he exclaimed, "Our experiments are doomed to success!" Well, we think these are examples of unethical uses of researchers and their methods. Funding agents and agencies – public or private – certainly may suggest to the researcher areas to be studied, questions to be answered, and hypotheses to be tested. But they should not pressure the researcher to produce data which appear to be economically or politically advantageous. This topic, sometimes referred to as the "Politics of Research," merits more intensive scrutiny than is intended here. One final thought: There are today certain taboo areas in research such as genetic engineering or the use of sexual surrogates. If work is carried on in these areas, the researcher may incur the wrath of certain pressure groups.

3

However, all this does not alter the fact that the researcher's work does involve ethical implications for his or her own conduct. This issue goes beyond mere courtesy and concerns the appropriate treatment of persons in a free society that values the dignity and worth of the individual. Such issues as invasion of privacy and the deception and manipulation of people require the researcher to accept ethical principles which will provide guidelines for proper conduct. The ethical researcher has obligations to his or her subjects, professional colleagues, and the public. This point will be treated again in Chapter #2.

Levels of Training in Research

The second major section of this chapter deals with <u>different levels of training in and doing research</u>. A primary concern of such training and another major objective of introductory courses like this is to achieve "<u>research literacy</u>." By that is meant the understanding of the research findings by consumers, professionals, and taxpayers. This understanding is based upon the ability to ask cogent questions pertaining to the formation of the problem, the selection of research tools, and the analysis of data. The questions which you should be asking may be found in the <u>Checklist for Evaluating a Research Report</u> in Appendix A. Hopefully, this course can help you find meaningful answers.

The next level of research ability is focused on becoming an "<u>action researcher</u>." At this level you are able to apply research methods to solving a problem which is of limited, local interest. You may whish to compare two different methods of teaching your students. Someone else may wish to ascertain ways of improving interpersonal relations within a department of an industrial concern. Action research attempts to deal with problems of limited scope and concern. No attempt is or should be made to generalize to situations beyond your own. The outcome of the study involving two different teaching methods may or may not be the same as found by someone else. That is unimportant. You are learning research skills which can be applied in answering questions which are of interest to you, your school, your department head, your city planning board, etc. These skills are learned in an introductory methods course such as this by either writing a detailed research proposal or by completing a micro-research project. A research proposal is a thorough piece of work which requires completion of all the research steps except the collection and analysis of the data.

The micro-research project requires all the steps including data gathering and analysis, but is more limited in scope and purpose.

At this point it is important to indicate that most introductory research methods texts[2] discuss what might be called a hierarchy of levels of research. Action research, as just indicated, is the least rigorous of these levels. At the other extreme is pure or basic research. Here we have a type of analysis designed to develop theories and principles which will add to man's store of knowledge about the world and universe. Some call this developing knowledge for the sake of knowledge with little or no concern for immediate practical applications. Some examples are deep space exploration and studies in theoretical genetics or perhaps a historical study designed to identify and explain how Horace Mann became interested in education.

Between these two levels is another level of research, usually labeled applied research. This level has many of the characteristics of basic research, including sampling techniques and, most important, inferences to the larger population. However, its purpose is to solve an immediate problem or improve a product or a process. For example, most educational research is applied research, for it attempts to develop generalizations about teaching-learning processes and instructional materials. Much of this kind of research has been done in the areas of administration and supervision, promotion and retention, the special child, and education in foreign languages, reading, math, and science.

An expansion of research on this level was accomplished during the 1960's through the Federal government's creation and support of Research and Development Centers, Regional Education Laboratories and Education Resources Information Centers (ERIC). It was hoped that these agencies would make the dissemination of research findings and products more effective and thus cut down the gap between what was known and what was implemented. (See Chapter #3 for more details of these agencies.)

Understanding something of the levels of research should help you to see better how your project fits in the total picture. Hopefully, it will also help you understand more clearly the various types of research approaches available for solving a problem. The three board

---

[2] See Best (1993), Gall, Borg, and Gall (1996), and Tuckman (1994).

categories most often identified are the historical-documentary (Chapter #6), descriptive (chapter #7), and experimental (Chapter #8).

It may also be helpful at this time to make a distinction between research and evaluation. While evaluation is also a systematic process for gathering data, it is most often thought of as a more holistic and naturalistic enterprise whose aim is to make a decision about some person, program, or situation. It is holistic because it is insufficient simply to study and measure only parts of a situation or to delimit to just certain variables and techniques. Rather, the evaluator attempts to gather data on all parts of the setting or object under study so as to understand it in totality. It is naturalistic in that it takes place in the field as a natural occurrence. The evaluator does not attempt to manipulate the phenomena understudy or their settings. The stress is on dealing with real world decision makers in helping them make the best judgment based on the most complete evidence. Thus to have direct impact.

Some basic evaluation questions are: Should this student be promoted, retained, or placed in a special section? Should this program be changed, eliminated, or continued? The following verbal equation may help clarify the meaning of evaluation:

Evaluation =

Quantitative techniques (tests, questionnaires, scales)

+

Quantitative techniques (observation, anecdotal records, interviews)

+

Professional judgment

As noted in the above description, evaluation consists of making decisions based on broad range of data gathered by both numerical and verbal techniques. Research, in contrast, tends to answer specific questions or test certain hypotheses. It tends to be more manipulative, controlled and delimited, and thus tends to have an indirect impact in contrast to the direct impact of evaluation.

If research excites you sufficiently, you may wish to become a professional researcher and thus achieve the highest level of training and doing research. It seems safe to say that industry, education, government and private agencies, to mention a few, will always require the services of professional researchers. In order to acquire research positions, especially upper level ones, additional and more specialized training is obviously required.

Some Research Terms

In reading your text, statistics booklet, worksheets, and research articles, and while listening to class discussions and presentations, you will come across terms which are strange to you. That is natural. Like other fields of study, research abounds with specialized terms or jargon. You need not memorize them. On page 9, you will find <u>Research Terms – A Selected List</u>. Refer to this list to check whether you have understood certain ideas and concepts discussed in your readings or in these lectures. The terms in and of themselves are not important, but the concepts which they represent are. We hope you will use the list as a tool for developing a better understanding of these terms as the course progresses. These technical words may be thought of as a kind of language barrier which can be overcome by looking them up, asking and thinking about them as they become important in the sequence of course topics.

Let us look at the term "operational definition" as an example. Under item #4 of the <u>Format of the Proposal for a Research Project</u> (Appendix B) you will find the subheading "Operational Definitions." It says here: "Clearly define the key variables, concepts, and terms which have a special meaning in your proposed study. Do not include mere semantic definitions." An operational definition is a precise, working definition. One type of operational definition is one which must be expressed in behavioral or measurable terms. If a researcher uses the construct "intelligence" in a study, "intelligence" must be defined in terms of scores on a specific test, perhaps the Wechsler Adult Intelligence Scale. For example, if the study deals with the gifted, a gifted student might be defined as one who scores 130 or above on some I. Q. test. In the same way, such terms as "self-concept" or "racial attitudes" must be defined with respect to specific measurement tools, such as the Tennessee Self-Concept Scale or the Situational Attitude Scale. Researchers who hypothesize that one instructional technique is more effective than another must define the term "effective" with reference to gains on specific criterion tests.

Another category of terms that may need definition contains those words of a highly technical nature. Here the writer must make an assumption and value judgment regarding the knowledge and expertise of the probable audience. Obviously every technical word can't be defined. However, those that would appear to be beyond the scope of the typical person reading the proposal probably should be.

A third category of terms that need definition contains those apparently common words with a very special meaning in your study. For example, Thomas Harris, in his bestseller I'm OK – You're OK, uses the technique of "author's note" placed before his preface to emphasize the unique meaning of "Parent," "Adult" and "Child" in his book. To Harris, each person has three states of being which are not roles but psychological realities; i.e. the personality is made up of the Parent, Adult and Child. Another example would be "high school." Again, this term seems quite clear, yet there are different kinds of high schools: vocational high schools, academic high schools, general high schools, 8-12 high schools, 10-12 high schools, etc. What exactly is the type dealt with in your study? So ask yourself what common words you might be using uncommonly.

There is one practical way of knowing whether a certain term must be defined. Ask yourself whether someone else reading your proposal clearly understands what you mean by that particular term. If the answer is "no," then spell it out clearly. A researcher, unlike a politician, must be precise. Research is one field where flowery rhetoric will do more harm than good.

Research Terms – A Selected List

Orientation
operational definition
"basic" vs. "applied" research
cross-sectional vs. longitudinal
　　　study

Use of Previous Research
ERIC

Statistics and Data Processing
population vs. sample
observation
test of significance
level of significance
null hypothesis
research hypothesis
normal curve
mean, median, mode
standard deviation
variance
semi-interquartile range
range
percentile
standard score (e.g. z-score)
correlation coefficient
analysis of variance
analysis of covariance
t-test
Chi Square
discrete vs. continuous data
computer program
primary vs. auxiliary data

Measurement
validity (content, concurrent, face,
　　　predictive, construct)
reliability (internal consistency,
　　　equivalency, stability)
standard error of measurement
Spearman-Brown prophesy formula
response set
criterion-referenced test
norm-referenced test
Kuder Richardson Formula No.21
Test blueprint

Types of Research
variable (independent,
　　　dependent, intervening)
cross-validation (replication)
experimental group(s)
control groups(s)
design (experimental design)
Hawthorne effect
error of fractionation
hypothesis (vs. assumption)
"treatment"
sample (random, systematic,
　　　cluster, stratified,
　　　convenient)
internal and external criticism
internal and external validity
primary vs. secondary sources
status study
casual-comparative study
correlational study
case study
content analysis
quasi-experiment

Methods of Research
halo effect
participant vs. non-participant
　　　observation
time sampling
generosity error
error of central tendency
contrast error
non-directive (depth) interview
interview guide
open-ended questions
non-projective test (vs.
　　　projective test)
"in-basket" technique
ATT Assessment Center
situational test
semantic differential
unobtrusive measures

Exercises for Chapter #1

1. How can research be succinctly defined?

2. Illustrate how Dewey's schema undergirds some modern research and teaching methodologies.

3. <u>Why</u> do we use research (methods/techniques/tools) instead of certain alternatives?

4. <u>How</u> should research be properly used (i.e. for which objectives)?
   <u>How</u> can research be misused (the "ethics" of research)?

5. Which research studies have given us fairly dependable information?
   (Give examples.)

6. Which research studies have <u>not</u> given us, at this time, dependable information?
   (Why not? What are some of the difficulties in doing research?)

7. To what extent is there "politics" in research? How can we cope with it?
   (Give examples.)

8. What are current "taboo" areas in research? Should research be carried out in these areas?

9. What are the three levels of research training? To which so you aspire? At which level will the research project you do in this course fall?

10. What is the difference between a research proposal and a micro-research project?

11. What are some different categories of research?

12. How can the various research laboratories and development centers be of help?

13. What are some differences between research and evaluation?

14. How do you define "operationally:" reading achievement, job satisfaction, high school, fast learner? Think of other terms in your field which may need to be defined operationally.

#2: Selection and Formulation of a Research Problem

This second chapter is divided into four sections: (1) sources for ideas to find a research problem; (2) criteria for selecting a research problem; (3) delimiting the research problem; and (4) research and value judgments.

Sources for Ideas

If you are a curious and inquisitive person, you may have wondered about a number of problems encountered in your profession. Are all kinds of aspirin equally effective? Is programmed instruction effective with certain kinds of students? Are certain gasoline additives living up to the advertisers' claims? What are the factors that brought about the growth and development of the guidance department in you school system? Are Distar and i. t. a. effective methods of teaching reading? A good staring point when shopping for and idea is your own experience and your own observations. These could be sources for questions to be studied or hypotheses to be tested. Research will then be a systematic way of following through on your hunches, which were derived from your needs and interests. Rather than only speculating about the relative virtues of different teaching methods, you can design a study which will demonstrate, at least in your situation, whether one method is better than another. Perhaps the following formula will be helpful: Experience + observation + needs + interests = research problem.

Systematic reading in the professional literature of your field will also aid you in locating a researchable problem. Frequently, investigators offer suggestions for further research when discussing the results of their study. Also, semi-professional magazines like Psychology Today and Discover are valuable sources. They are also interesting reading because they tend to steer away from jargon. Others have also found reading popular magazines like The Reader's Digest quite rewarding. In these magazines, technical subjects are often discussed in a comprehensible manner. If you are ready to be stimulated, these magazines can be a great help. Another excellent way of getting started is looking over recent convention programs of your professional organization which will acquaint you with the most recent research efforts in various specialty areas. Since there are often extensive delays between the completion of a research study and its publication in journals and inclusion in indexes and abstracts, perusal of convention programs is most highly recommended. Are you still at a loss as how to locate a researchable problem? If so, another possibility is doing a replication project. That is, adapt (not adopt) a study already done to fit your needs. This can be justified due to passage of time, different location, correcting weaknesses and limitations pointed out in the study.

Criteria for Selecting a Research Problem

After you have tentatively identified an area for investigation, we suggest that you apply certain criteria before you commit yourself too deeply. These are:

1. sustained motivation
2. adequate training and personal predilections
3. feasibility
4. importance to your profession.

The undertaking of a research study is a time-consuming task, and therefore you should be highly motivated to embark upon one. Are you really interested in the topic which you have chosen or has someone talked you into it? Be honest with yourself and determine whether you are really excited about what you wish to study. Will it have some practical value in helping you in your job or developing your career?

Is it right in light of your training and personal preferences? Some research problems are more complex than others. Do you have enough training to undertake a certain study? An evaluation of a total program, such as Career Education, requires a fairly sophisticated plan of action called the "research design." On the other hand, evaluating the effectiveness of the Tungsten-Hydro-Catalyst, a gasoline saving device, would be a less difficult task. While you may avail yourself of professional assistance in planning and conducting your research study, you should be able to manage most of it yourself. Also, as pointed out in Chapter #1, there are different types of research and a multitude of methods and tools. Since these will be discussed in more detail in later chapters, let us again mention them briefly here. There is historical (dealing with the past), descriptive (dealing with the present), and experimental (dealing with the future) research. A study may focus on human beings, animals, written documents, materials, TV programs, etc. Tools such as an observation, interview, questionnaire or test, to cite a few, may be used. Which type of research appeals to you? Do you wish to study people on a semi-personal basis? Or do you prefer a topic requiring less personal involvement such as the content analysis of certain textbooks or TV programs? Are you impatient to get fairly immediate results or do you have the patience to wait? How high is your frustration tolerance? Evaluate yourself and then decide what to do.

Is it feasible for you? You may be excited about a certain research problem and feel that you are able to work on it. Now ask yourself if your proposed study is *feasible.* Do you have sufficient time to carry it out? You may have to meet certain deadlines at the college or on your job. Your problem may have to be delimited or narrowed down. Do you have access to subjects? If special equipment or research tools are needed, are these available or must they first be developed? Very often institutional sponsorship and cooperation are important. For instance, a study of alumni would be facilitated if a school or college will allow use of its letterhead on the transmittal letter. One cannot study school children or industrial workers unless the cooperation of school authorities or front office management is assured. Then again, a study may not be feasible because the hazards inherent in gathering the data are too great.   The need to protect the privacy of individuals may be a crippling handicap when embarking upon research in certain sensitive human areas. Now, one final example of a factor which may rule out a research study: A problem may simply be too complex for investigation at the present time. There may be too many variables to be considered, or reliable and valid tools may not yet exist which would be needed to tackle a given problem. Can you offer examples of intriguing and important problems which seem too difficult to be resolved via research at the present time? One example that comes to mind is the study of "effective" teachers.   After more than 60 years of intensive study by thousands of investigators, we still cannot identify and describe "effective" teachers. What is "effective" and what is meant by "teaching?" Which criteria of "effective" teaching are relevant and to whom? Which other non-school related factors affect behavior, rightly or wrongly attributed to teaching? Are teachers to be evaluated in terms of short or long-range goals? "Teaching" itself is a many-splendored thing, a very complex process, difficult to assess. Is it realistic to study "teaching effectiveness?" Some believe that this area is not researchable today and for a long time to come.   This conclusion may be frustrating, but then not all problems are researchable.

Is it important to your profession? Finally, the last criterion asks the question: Is the proposed project of some value to your profession? Does it add to our store of information? Does it, in your opinion, provide fresh insights for some of your colleagues? We do not say that your study has to be entirely original. If it is, so much the better. However, as indicated earlier, you may make a contribution to your field by replicating a study. For instance, social class differences with respect to child rearing have been studied at fairly regular intervals. Shifts in practices among people of different socioeconomic class structures are interesting to note. Also, every ten years or so someone finds it useful to ascertain the status rankings of 50 or so occupations. Perhaps the results are useful to guidance counselors. Studies of sexual attitudes and mores seem to be fashionable to replicate in every generation. Many studies have been done on reading methods.

Delimiting the Research Problem

Let us suppose that you have located an interesting, feasible, and worthwhile area for investigation. Your next step is to delimit your problem – that is, to narrow a general idea down to one that is manageable by you. There is no magic way to accomplish this. However, the best way is to read extensively in the literature related to your field of interest. By reading the research studies of investigators in your field of interest, you will learn what has been done and what problems were encountered by them. You will be introduced to methods which are potentially useful to you and you will get ideas for researchable problems. Since you are a neophyte, you may wish to seek assistance from your instructor so that your general problem or area of interest can be translated into a specific, manageable problem. See Chapters #6, 7, and 8 for specific examples of research problems, questions and hypotheses.

There is usually some confusion in the minds of beginning researchers in distinguishing between delimitations and limitations. A delimitation may be thought of as a premeditated limitation. That is, the researcher deliberately narrows down, excludes and is selective with all subjects, sources, and techniques. It may also be that some delimitations are too severe and turn out to be limitations. Thus, a limitation is a weakness in the study which becomes apparent during or after its completion. Of course, there are other causes of weakness.

Delimitations generally include some of the following specific categories: (1) the number of observations, subjects or cases; e.g., this investigation is delimited to senior high school boys; (2) time and geographic location; e.g., this study is delimited to fifth grade children in Essex County for a three-year period; (3) the selection of sources, especially in historical-documentary research; e.g., this study is delimited to selected libraries, information retrieval systems and basic sources like the recent annual issues of the English Journal, etc. Finally, sometimes it is helpful to narrow down the topic by telling what the study is not. For example, if the researcher proposes to do a study of a man and his work by stating that the study will not be a biography of the man's life, the intent of the study is clarified.

Research and Value Judgments

This presentation on problem selection would not be complete without some reference to moral issues facing the modern researcher. Many laymen and researchers regard research as amoral – that is, not implicated with value issues. We tend to disagree, as we indicated in Chapter #1. A researcher wittingly or not does make value judgments. These, hopefully, are ethically sound.

Value judgments or ethical considerations enter into: (1) the selection of a problem; (2) the selection of methods; (3) the interpretation of data; (4) the reporting of findings; (5) concern for the application of findings. How can one demonstrate the validity of this assertion? For example, by focusing on one area rather than another, the researcher (in effect) makes a value judgment. Whereas one researcher chooses to deal with cancer research, others opt for potentially controversial areas such as genetic engineering. The selection of proper methods for investigation, such as providing safeguards for human and animal subjects, is often regulated by professional codes of ethics (see APA, 1982). In addition, researchers may be tempted to interpret their data selectively, such as choosing to ignore so-called "non-significant" findings. Moreover, researchers may choose whether or not to report their findings to fellow professionals and to laymen. By selecting certain journals, researchers can effectively withhold information from laymen. Some investigators may feel that it is beneath their dignity to be published in mass circulation magazines. Finally, researchers may or may not feel responsible for the ultimate application of their findings. Does their responsibility end with the publication of their studies? We believe that a researcher should not operate within a social vacuum and cannot avoid making value judgments. Hopefully, these are morally sound and contribute to the betterment of the "human condition."

1. What are some obstacles which may discourage a person from undertaking research?

2. List a few important and intriguing problems which you feel are too difficult to be resolved via research at the present time. Why do you think so?

3. Which studies do you think are worthy of replication today? Why did you select these studies?

4. Your research problem

    a) What is your area of interest?

    b) Where could you look for help in deciding upon a specific research problem?

    c) What criteria will you apply when deciding upon a specific research problem?

    d) What criteria can be applied to narrow down or delimit a research problem? What is the distinction between a limitation and a delimitation?

    e) How might your value judgments affect your research endeavors?

#3: Use of Previous Research

In this third chapter we shall discuss with you: (1) reasons for reviewing research related to your chosen problem; (2) bibliographic aids and preliminary sources of information; (3) library research techniques and sources of information; (4) criteria for analyzing a research report; and (5) writing the section "Related Research" for your research proposal.

Reasons for Reviewing Research Related to your Problem

It is quite unlikely that you were the first person to be interested in your topic for research. Therefore, it seems reasonable that you could benefit from the efforts of other investigators who have worked in your area. Thus, the two primary purposes of reviewing the related literature are to help you attack your specific problem and to develop a collective point of reference in discussing and interpreting your findings. Specifically, this review can: (1) help you delimit your problem; (2) introduce you to new approaches toward solving your problem; (3) help you avoid errors in planning your study; (4) suggest new ideas to you; and (5) acquaint you with new sources of data. Can you think of other reasons why you should invest time in reading studies in the area related to your current interest?

You may wonder, in looking for material, how far afield you should go. First, in regard to library and other information services, we recommend the use of more that one of these facilities. It is true that you need not fly to Washington, DC and use the Library of Congress. On the other hand, delimiting yourself to the college/university library may turn out to be too severe a limitation. Second, when dealing with specific sources, suppose someone wishes to evaluate a certain number of social studies textbooks used in the Happytown School District for evidence of sex role stereotyping. Which topics do you think could yield related research? The primary target would be studies under the same heading. Then studies which report evaluations in subject areas other than social studies should be reviewed. Also, since "sex role stereotyping" is not a simple concept – that is, one cannot easily defined and measured – studies bearing on this concept should be looked over. Undoubtedly, studies have been undertaken on "sex role stereotyping" with a focus other than its prevalence in textbooks. To round out the presentation of related research, studies which report on changing sex roles as reflected in the home, in industry, or in the community could be included. Generally, it is better to read a little farther afield than to limit one's search for material at the outset. Also, it is important to note that this selection of types of sources lays the groundwork for the way you subgroup the body of the literature review.

Bibliographic Aids and Preliminary Sources of Information

Your search for related research is greatly facilitated by a number of bibliographic aids and sources which are available to you. In addition to the reference librarian, general bibliographic guides are excellent for obtaining information about library techniques and resources. One popular reference of this kind is the Bibliographic Guide to Educational Research by Dorothea Berry. This guide comprises an annotated bibliography of reference works in the field of education which includes chapters on research studies, government publications, special materials and how to write a research paper. This book and similar bibliographic guides in other fields can be important preliminary sources for the researcher.

Library Research Techniques and Sources of Information

At this stage of your education, you have probably developed your own techniques of doing library research. If you are still open to suggestions, consider the following pointers.

1. List the synonyms and alternate search terms of key concepts in your study. For instance, information relating to "self-concept" may be found under the headings "self-image," "self-perception," "perception, self" or "attitudes, toward self." Users of ERIC are well advised first to consult the Thesaurus of ERIC Descriptors. It contains the subject headings and descriptors under which ERIC documents are indexed. See Appendix C for a list of ERIC clearinghouses designed to collect and catalog research information from different professional areas.

ERIC was one of only several agencies that were first funded by the Federal government in the late 1960's when it greatly expanded its support of education and educational research. Much important work in educational research and development has been done by a number of laboratories and development centers located in college and university settings around the country. These, too, could be excellent sources of information for the researcher. A complete directory can be obtained from the Council for Educational Development and Research, 1518 K Street, NW, Washington, D.C. 20005.

2. Next, consult preliminary sources, such as indexes and abstract, rather than going directly to journals. Important sources in the fields of psychology and education are the Psychological Abstracts, the Education Index, the Current Index to Journals in Education, and the Social Science Index. The sources will refer you to articles which are germane to your study. Comparable indexes and abstracts exist in other fields of study. All of these titles are now available on CD-ROM.

3. The use of one or more database information retrieval systems will greatly facilitate access to previous research and thus minimize the need for time-consuming manual searches.

CD-ROMs (Compact Disk-Read Only Memory) are available for use in most academic and in many public libraries. Some of the most frequently used CD-ROMs are ERIC, Psyc Lit, Social Sciences Index, General Science Index and ABI-INFORM. Access to CD-ROM databases is usually free.

Other access to several hundred on line databases, including Dissertation Abstracts, is available through DIALOG Information Services and BRS Bibliographic Retrieval Services.

Students are usually asked to fill out a search request form for an on-line search and the search is done by a librarian. Check with your academic and public library to see what is available, who is eligible to use the service and what the fees are.

Numerous printed indexes are also available in machine-readable form. By utilizing a computer terminal, a librarian or bibliographic searcher can retrieve information from a variety of databases encompassing many subject areas in a relatively short time. These databases are updated more frequently than printed indexes.

4. Accurate and complete note-taking is essential when reviewing research materials. We suggest that you do at least two things. First of all, make a bibliographic card by using a 3 x 5 index card for each reference. On that card, record the complete reference. Again, examples of complete references and note-taking techniques are available in most introductory research methods texts. Second, use a separate sheet of notebook paper of a 5 x 8 index card for each reference. On this, record systematically for all important sources:

Author and title (keyed to your 3 x 5 index card)

Problem (hypotheses and/or questions posed)

Method used (population, sample, research design, technique of measurement)

Findings (major as well as minor)

Conclusions

Implications

Your comments regarding limitations and noteworthy features, etc.

If you are selecting a quotation or paraphrasing, be certain to record the page reference.

Criteria for Analyzing a Research Report

In the first chapter we referred to the achievement of "research literacy" as a major objective of an introductory research methods course. Implicit here is an understanding of research findings and the ability to ask and answer certain crucial questions pertaining to a given research report. In order to help you ask the right questions. We have prepared a Checklist for Evaluating a Research Report (see Appendix A). If you can say "yes" to most items comprising the checklist when critically reviewing a research study, then you have found a pretty solid piece of research. However, if you are forced to say "no" to most items, then the research study is of dubious value. See the end of chapter activities for an exercise in evaluating a research study.

Take this checklist along when you are reading research studies and keep these questions in mind when you are reacting to and recording what you are reading. Then you will be able to present a critical review of related research, not just a summary of the findings.

Writing the Section "Related Research"
For Your Research Proposal

Please turn now to the Format of the Proposal for a Research Project in Appendix B and reread Section #3.

A. In order to present related research for descriptive and experimental studies effectively and meaningfully, please do the following:

1. Present a critical review of these studies. Report sufficient information (i.e. the problem, method, findings, conclusions, virtues and drawbacks) so that your reader knows what the study was all about and to what extent it is a good piece of research.

2. Show how these studies relate to your problem, your hypotheses and/or questions, and your procedure.

3. Group related research under <u>common</u> topical headings. That is, organize the section titled "Related Research" into headings under which studies relating to a common theme or time period are reported.

4. Try to integrate the work of several researchers when they have studied a similar problem, used similar techniques, or arrived at similar conclusions. For example:

> Smith (1997, Jones (1996) and Smart (1995) have studied self-concepts of adolescents. Smith (1997) and Smart (1995) administered Lang's Checklist of Traitnames, while Jones (1996) used Short's Sentence Completion Test.

First present the elements common to these authors; then deal with them separately, as needed. Good examples of what we are talking about may be found in the <u>Annual Review of Psychology</u> as well as in annual reviews of other subject areas. Also, consult the <u>Review of Educational Research</u> and the <u>Psychological Bulletin</u>.

5. Conclude the "Related Research" section with a succinct summary containing major generalizations regarding the content and methods of the studies reviewed and how these relate to your project.

B. In order to present a proper review of the related literature in <u>historical</u>, <u>documentary</u>, <u>bibliographical</u> and <u>construction</u> type projects, do the following:

1. Begin with a brief introduction indicating library and preliminary sources used and what subheadings you are using to categorize the body of the review.

2. Present the thesis and a brief outline of the content of the source. Your notes may include quotes, paraphrases, summaries, or more evaluative treatment as suggested above for statistical type studies.

3. Group the literature according to what seem to be logical common topical headings and chronological periods. There should be a clear-cut connection between these subtopics, the basic questions you wanted answered, and the tentative table of contents of your finished product.

4. Show how these sources are related to your problem and procedure. What do you expect to get from them? <u>Remember</u>, in this kind of research the literature <u>is your</u>

data; so don't get into extensive analysis now. Students have a tendency to present the findings, but this is more like writing a term paper than doing a research project.

5. Conclude with a brief summary indicating the principal levels, categories, and specific types of sources to be used.

See also Chapter #6 for more details.

Exercises for Chapter #3

1. List reasons other than those stated in the chapter for investing time in reading studies in the area related to your field of interest.

2. Look over the <u>Checklist for Evaluating a Research Report</u> and indicate which items you feel are of <u>primary</u> importance and of <u>secondary</u> importance. Why? Select a research article for review and evaluation. Follow the checklist and record your reactions on separate sheets of paper.

3. Investigate the ERIC system. Identify key concepts and search terms of your study and consult the <u>Thesaurus of ERIC Descriptors</u>. Locate the relevant ERIC documents.

4. Compare your library research techniques with those listed in this chapter. How does your technique differ? Which weakness, if any, do you feel should be corrected?

5. Determine the particular style of citing references which is used in your discipline. (Look over your professional journals and seminar reports written by people in your field.)

6. Determine the particular style of handling the literature review in your discipline. Compare it with the suggestions made in the last part of this chapter for writing the "Review of Literature" section of your proposal.

#4: Statistical Analyses and Data Processing

Anyone embarking upon a descriptive or experimental research study will undertake some kind of statistical analysis. Statistics are also used to determine the validity and reliability[1] of research instruments. Moreover, some historical documentary research studies involve the use and presentation of statistical data. Thus statistical literacy is essential to do and to use most kinds of research.

A researcher who is statistically literate should be able to:
1. Know which statistical tools are available
2. Determine which kind of data require the use of which tool
3. Compute certain statistics when manual calculations are desired
4. Interpret statistical data and prepare them for presentations
5. Communicate intelligently with specialists in data processing
6. Prepare statistical data for processing

We will not present in this chapter the statistical computations of their interpretations.
For these the reader is referred to a supplementary source such as A Practical Guide to Statistics for Research and Measurement (Lang) or Simplified Statistics (Koenker).

The researcher should consider very early while developing a research problem which statistical tools are to be used. This should be done when the hypotheses and/or questions are being formulated. One should certainly not collect the data first and then ponder what to do with them. Statistical tools are part of the research design, or plan of operation, and require careful consideration prior to launching the study.

Kinds of Data

There are two kinds of data – continuous and discrete (i.e. categorical). Continuous data consist of scores which can fall along a continuum. Discrete (categorical) data consist of responses in distinct categories. Continuous data are, for example, scores on tests,

---

[1] Validity and reliability will be discussed in Chapter #5.

physical measurements, temperature readings, etc. Examples of categorical data are responses on a structured questionnaire (__ lower class; __ middle class; __ upper class) or on an interview ("Are you happy today?" __ Yes; __ No; __ Don't know). Different kinds of statistical tools are appropriate for the two kinds of data. For <u>continuous</u> data, the researcher may use statistics such as the mean ($\overline{X}$), the median (Mdn), the standard deviation (SD), the semi-interquartile range (Q), the correlation coefficient (r or R), the <u>t</u>- test, or the <u>F</u>-ratio. When dealing with <u>discrete</u> (categorical) data, the researcher may simply list the frequencies (f) or compute percentages (%), or perhaps use Chi Square (χ^2). The researcher must decide: (1) which type of data to collect – continuous or discrete or perhaps both; and (2) which specific statistic to use for given type of data.

The researcher deals with two branches of statistics – <u>descriptive statistics</u> and <u>inferential statistics</u>.

Descriptive Statistics

Descriptive statistics are concerned with the description of a group of individuals and summarize what is typical or characteristic of a particular group. What is the average salary of workers in the Quitearly Factory? How homogeneous is Ms. Mann's class with respect to reading ability? How does Ken compare with the rest of his class? To what extent is noise related to population density? Questions like these get at descriptions of a sample.

The four basic types of descriptive statistics are:

<u>Measures of Central Tendency</u> (e.g. What is the average salary of workers in the Quitearly Factory?).

<u>Measures of Variability</u> (e.g. What percentage of workers earn salaries within certain ranges?).

<u>Measures of Relative Position</u> (e.g. How does Ken's salary compare with those of his fellow workers?).

<u>Measures of Correlation</u> (e.g. How does job tenure relate to salary earned?).

Measures of Central Tendency

These measures give us an idea of the typical or representative score around which other scores tend to cluster. Three commonly used measures or statistics are: the mean (arithmetic), the median, and the mode.

The (arithmetic) <u>mean</u> is the average obtained by adding together all of the scores in a set and dividing by the number of scores. It is used when the distribution of scores is fairly symmetrical about the center and when other statistics will be obtained which use the mean as part of the formula (for example, the z-score).

The <u>median</u> is the middle score in a distribution or set of ranked scores. It divides the group of scores into two equal parts. The median is also known as the 50th percentile. The median is calculated when the score distribution is asymmetrical (i.e. lopsided) and thus the mean would give a misleading picture. For instance, if most factory workers earn salaries in the $9,000 - $30,000 range and the company president earns $200,000, then the mean salary of all employees (including the president) will give a distorted picture. On the other hand, the median – which is not affected by one of more extreme scores (e.g. the president's salary) – will be more representative of the typical salary of the employees of the Quitearly Factory.

The <u>mode</u> is the score which occurs most frequently in a set of scores. It is thus a quick estimate of the typical of representative score and may also be helpful in interpreting the mean and median.

Measure of Variability

These statistics tell us something about the clustering of scores around the typical or representative score. They indicate the degree of homogeneity or heterogeneity of a group. The more the scores vary or deviate from the typical score, the more heterogeneous is the group. Three commonly used measures or statistics of variability are: the standard deviation, the semi-interquartile range, and the range.

The complementary statistics of central tendency (the typical score) and variability (degree of homogeneity) are: mean and standard deviation; median and semi-interquartile range; and mode and range. Thus, if the mean is the appropriate statistic denoting the "typical" score, then the standard deviation is the appropriate statistic denoting variability. On the other hand, if the researcher opts for the median, then the semi-interquartile range should be computed as an indication of variability.

The standard deviation (SD) expresses the dispersion of scores around the mean. The more the scores cluster close around the mean, the smaller is the standard deviation. In a normal, bell-shaped distribution, about two-thirds of the scores are within the range from one SD below to one SD above the mean.

The semi-interquartile range (Q) denotes the dispersion of scores around the median. Fifty percent of the scores are included within the limits: median plus and minus Q.

The range, the quick estimate of variability, represents the difference between the highest and lowest score in a set.

Measures of Relative Position

These measures or statistics allow us to compare the score of one person with those of others, all belonging to the same group (e.g. How well did Jane do in spelling compared to her classmates?). Also, we can compare the scores obtained by one person on different tests (e.g. Did Jane do better in spelling than in algebra or social studies?). Percentiles and various kinds of standard scores (e.g. z-scores, T-scores, and stanines) are used to express a person's relative position.

A percentile is a point or score which indicates the percentage of persons who scored below that point. Thus, if a score of 45 is the 50th percentile (P_{50} = Median), then one-half of all persons in a certain group scored below 45. If a score of 32 corresponds to the 25th percentile (P_{25}), then 25 percent of all persons in that group scored below 32.

A standard score is a transformed score into which an original raw score may be expressed. For instance, the z-score denotes how may standard deviation units a person's raw score deviates from the mean of the group to which he/she belongs (e.g. z = 2.0 means that Jane's score on the spelling test places her 2 SD – standard deviation – units above the mean of her class; z = -1.5 means that her score on the social studies test places her 1 ½ SD units below the mean of her class).

Statistics expressing the relative position of test scores are used for the setting up of test norms – i.e. frames of reference for the interpretation of test scores. Test constructors and researchers tend to prefer standard scores (such as the z-score) over percentiles because the latter do not provide equal units of measurement. Standard scores <u>do</u> represent equal units of measurement, the SD being the <u>common</u> basis for comparing scores derived from different kinds of tests.

<u>Measures of Correlation</u>

This group of statistics enables us to study relationships among variables and is thus widely used in research and testing. The researcher should select from among a number of correlational methods the one which is most suitable. There are methods which are appropriate for all kinds of data, continuous and discrete (categorical). For instance, the correlation between scores on the Wechsler Adult Intelligence Scale and the Emes Test of Creativity (both variables are expressed as continuous data) may be ascertained via the product-moment or rank-difference method. The analysis of questionnaire, interview, or attitude scale items (usually reflecting discrete data) may be handled via Chi Square (χ^2). For instance, this method could be used when determining how generally "optimistic" or "pessimistic" people compare in their responses to the statement: "The crucial problems facing our country can be solved" (when the response options are "agree," "disagree," or "don't know").

Detailed presentations of correlational methods and their interpretation may be found in Lang (1993), Downie and Heath (1983), and Bruning and Kintz (1990).

Two cautions should be mentioned here: (1) The continuous variables to be correlated need <u>not</u> have the same units – i.e. we can correlate "height" (Variable X, expressed in inches) with "weight" (Variable Y, expressed in pounds), or "noise" (expressed in decibels) with "distance" (expressed in feet). (2) The existence of a high correlation between the two variables (X and Y) does not <u>necessarily</u> indicate that either X or Y has any causal influence on the other. An increase in the number of subway police (X) was found to correlate very highly with an increase in subway crimes (Y). Does X cause Y or vice versa? Most likely, an increase in population (Variable Z) is associated with an increase in X as well as Y. Or, if intelligence (X) is positively correlated with numbers of visits to physicians (Y), can we conclude that more intelligent people are sicker than less intelligent ones? Of course not.

Statistical Inference

Statistical inference is a branch of statistics which deals with the generalization from a sample (or samples) to a population (or populations) and involves the testing of hypotheses. Generalizations (from sample to population) can only be made if the sample has been <u>randomly</u> selected.[2]

Five commonly used procedures in statistical inference are:[3]

1. <u>t-test for significance of the difference between independent (uncorrelated) means</u>
This <u>t</u>-test is used when one whishes to compare two <u>different</u> groups. <u>Example</u>: Men and women were administered the Attitudes Toward Martians Scale. The <u>t</u>-test will tell us whether the mean attitudes of men differ significantly (at the .05 level) from those of women.

2. <u>t-test for significance of difference between correlated means</u>
This <u>t</u>-test, using a different formula than the one in 1., is applied when one whishes to compare pre- and post-treatment scores of the people in one (the same) group. <u>Example</u>: A group of women was administered the Attitudes Toward Martians Scale prior to their trip to Mars. The trip to Mars is regarded here as the "treatment." Upon their return to Earth, they again responded to this scale. This <u>t</u>-test is used to ascertain the significance of the difference between mean pre-treatment scores (i.e. prior to their trip) and mean post-treatment scores.

3. <u>Analysis of variance (one-way) – one variable study</u>

---

[2] Types of samples and related concepts will be discussed in Chapter #8.
[3] Bruning and Kintz (1990) present these and other procedures with step-by-step solutions. Computer programs exist for all commonly used statistical procedures.

The t-test is used when only two means are compared (either correlated or uncorrelated). If several means are to be compared, it is inefficient to compute a series of t-tests. One-way analysis of variance is the appropriate technique to be used when one wishes to ascertain the significance of the differences among several means. Example: Citizens of ten Earth nations are given the above-cited scale. The significance of the differences between the ten groups of citizens is ascertained via analysis of variance.

4. Analysis of variance (two-way) – two variable study

This method is used when an experimenter resorts to a factorial design in research. It is a fairly sophisticated technique and will be discussed more fully in Chapter #8. Example: An experimenter wishes to determine the effectiveness of an indoctrination program which is to result in more positive attitudes toward Martians. Groups of "young" and "old" women and men (called experimental groups) participate in these indoctrination sessions. Other groups of "young" and "old" women and men (called control groups) are part of the experiment but don't attend the sessions. Employing the two-way analysis of variance, we can answer questions such as these:

    a. Was the indoctrination program effective?

    b. Was the program more effective for men or for women?

    c. Was the program more effective for "young" or "old" persons?

5. Analysis of covariance

In an experimental pretest-posttest design, an effort is made to equate the experimental (E) and control (C) groups on a number of relevant variables either by random assignment or by matching. For instance, in a study of the effect of different methods of teaching reading, a relevant causal variable may be intelligence. Therefore, the experimenter would try to equate both E and C groups with respect to intelligence prior to the experiment. If this is impossible to do, like in a quasi-experiment, and the E and C groups differ initially with respect to intelligence, then the researcher must take this into consideration when analyzing the data. Analysis of covariance is the statistical technique which equates (statistically) members of the E and C groups with respect to intelligence. Thus, analysis of covariance is a post-hoc method of matching groups on variables, such as intelligence, which may affect the outcome of the study.

It is not our intention to treat analysis of variance, covariance, or any other multivariate analysis in any depth, but simply to alert you to the fact that these techniques exist. The computational routine for these techniques is usually handled by computer programs.

Essentially, the use of statistics in research involves a series of decisions and choices. We have tried to introduce you to this area and help you get started. Don't be discouraged if you find some of the material difficult. You are here to learn, so don't be afraid to ask questions.

Manual vs. Electronic Data Processing

We have suggested that the researcher decide during the planning phase which statistical tools will be used. Since statistical data need to be processed and analyzed, the prudent researcher will also think about data processing requirements prior to launching the study. The selection and design of research documents (e.g. answer sheets, questionnaires, etc.) is tied in with data processing (to be discussed later on), as are considerations of time, money, and the complexity of the research project. Consult with a data processing specialist to determine whether manual of electronic data processing is more appropriate for you If you opt for electronic processing, find out in which format the data should be turned over to the specialist and the format of the data which you will be getting. The technology used for data processing changes rapidly and you need the advice of an expert who keeps abreast of these changes.

The researcher may elect to compute the data manually when the study involves few cases, if simple statistics are needed, and if only one or two variables are involved. Very inexpensive hand held calculators are available which make it easy to calculate rather quickly means, standard deviations, and correlation coefficients. However, analyses of a number of variables or complex statistical procedures are generally performed cheaper, faster and more accurately by a computer. Even if the researcher opts for computerized data processing, some manual calculations can and may help the researcher get a "feel" for the data prior to getting the computer results and enable him/her to check the computer printout for errors. In addition, preliminary "hand" analysis of (pilot) data may reveal trends which might suggest changes in research design.

At the present time, most statistical analyses are performed on micro-computers which are relatively small and inexpensive, and may sometimes also be referred to as personal or home computers. These micro-computers are capable of performing a wide range of statistical analysis procedures ranging from calculation of sample means and variances to the most complex multivariate analyses. The choice of the appropriate statistical analysis programs to use on these computers is also an important area to discuss with a computer consultant prior to initiating a research project.

The three basic steps in analyzing data when using any computers are input, processing and output. Input may be accomplished via the use of data already stored on disks, or, it may be typed in through the keyboard. Processing is done in the central processing unit. This unit performs the arithmetical and logical operations on the data necessary to carry out the statistical instructions from the statistical analysis programs stored on disks in the computer.

The output step involves the transferring of data from the internal storage of the computer to an output device, usually a video screen, a floppy disk, or, if a hard copy is needed, a "printout" on computer paper.

See the steps in the Data Processing section of this chapter for more details in carrying out these steps.

While it is true that the large digital computer is one of the most versatile and ingenious developments of the middle twentieth century, micro-computer technology has grown so fast that both hardware and software are available which enable users to do virtually all of the statistical procedures that could previous be done only on mainframe computers. The term hardware must be understood to apply to any and all computer equipment, while the term software applies to the programs which instruct the hardware to perform specific tasks.

Micro-computers consist of four basic parts: Input devices, a Central Processing Unit (CPU), Memory and Mass Storage devices, and Output devices. Input Devices allow instructions and data to be entered into the central processor and consist primarily of keyboards, and RS-232 "Serial Communications Ports" which allow communication between any two computers via direct connection or over telephone lines (with the addition of a telephone "Modem"). Data may also be "input" from sets of numbers called files stored on floppy disks. The Central Processor (CPU) combines input information or instructions with programs or data stored in memory or other mass storage devices and sends the results to the output devices. Memory is usually contained in the CPU and may be of the Random-Access-Memory (RAM) type and/or Read-Only Memory (ROM) type. RAM is user-alterable memory which stores information temporarily until it is altered again, or until the computer is turned off. ROM cannot be altered and is used to store information like basic computer instructions permanently inside the computer. Memory size is measured in millions (M) of "words" called "bytes" (which correspond to single characters like numbers or letters). Thus, a computer with a 4M memory can store about 4,000,000 letters or numbers (about 800 single-spaced pages) in its memory. Some of this memory may be consumed by internal programs and thus, the term "usable memory" becomes important.

Mass Storage Devices allow storage of large amounts of data in semi-permanent form on flexible (floppy) or hard disks. Output Devices allow the computer to communicate with the user and include Video-Display-Terminals (VDT), printers of the dot-matrix, ink-jet or laser type, and RS-232 ports and telephone modems which allow the computer to send its data to other computers. Computer data and programs in the form of "bytes" (single letters or numbers) are usually coded as ASCII (American Standards Committee for Information Interchange) characters and transferred in this format. For a more in-depth description of micro-computer hardware and software, you may want to browse through the selection of sources in the computer section of any large bookstore.

Technological advances in the past few years have made computers and electronic data processing an integral part of any research effort. An ever increasing variety of computers and computer programs are available to facilitate efficient and accurate data analysis. The state-of-the-art is changing so rapidly that the neophyte researcher may not be aware of the most recent developments. Therefore, the neophyte researcher will find it most beneficial to consult a computer expert prior to embarking on a research project.

Computer Programs

A computer program is a set of instructions arranged in a step-by-step sequence which the computer employs to handle the data. A large number of programs have been developed (so-called canned programs) to cover all of the commonly used statistical procedures. Popular programs are: SAS (Statistical Analysis System), SPSS (Statistical Package for the Social Sciences), Data Text, and BMD (Biomedical Series). Check with your local computer center regarding the availability and appropriateness of programs.

Another important aspect of computer usage is word processing and desktop publishing. This type of software introduced a new dimension in manuscript preparation. Using a word processor, a person with some typing skills and a few days of training and practice, can handle the preparation of bibliographies, articles, newsletters, magazines, and books with increased speed and accuracy. It is possible to correct errors in spelling, punctuation, and sentence structure as well as reorganize parts and sections of the manuscript without retyping the original document. Entire pages, including graphics, can be prepared for publication directly on the computer screen. Thus one can move from first draft to error-free final copy by executing the rewriting and editorial tasks electronically and greatly simplify the whole process.

Computer programs also permit access to the Internet. The Internet provides access to an incredible variety of useful information. By typing in an address called a URL (Universal Resource Locator), the computer user can visit millions of libraries, universities, association databases and individuals throughout the world. By typing in the URL for a search service such as http://www.altavista.com, searches for any desired information, concept, or data stored anywhere in the world can be performed. By using Altavista or some other search service to search USENET, it is possible to locate groups of people who are interested in discussing virtually any topic that can be specified. The Internet is a very valuable source of information for all researchers and scientists.

Steps in Data Processing

Kinds of Research Instruments to be Processed

Diverse research instruments need to be analyzed, such as test answer sheets or cards, survey answer sheets, questionnaires, etc. The data recorded on some instruments need not be hand entered, but may be "read" directly by an optical scanner.

Give serious consideration to the use of such research instruments since the avoidance of keyboard entry of the data represents a tremendous saving in time and money. Instruments which require keyboard entry should be carefully designed to facilitate this task, as discussed later on. Some research projects can be performed on small laptop computers which administer the questions or stimuli to the subjects on their screens and record the subjects' responses directly on their keyboards. Thus, an entire experiment can be presented and analyzed on a portable computer.

Data Recording

Data should be recorded on a specially designed data sheet that can be optically scanned into the computer, if possible. If not, the data can be recorded on a data sheet for eventual keyboard entry into the computer. An example is the Space Travel Aptitude Test study (STAT). The data collected for this study may be listed on a data sheet as shown in Figure 1 (see page 36). Note that the columns show the variables and that each row lists the data for one person. Data sheets in the form of analysis pads can be purchased in various sizes.

The columns of the different data sheets represent different variables, but the first row of each sheet always lists the data of the first person; the second row lists the data of the second person; etc. The initial columns of every layout list the subject ID.

Suggestions

In conclusion, we suggest the following to help you save time and energy and avoid grief:

1. Consult with a data processing specialist prior to selecting or developing your research instrument.
2. Allow sufficient time for data processing if the data must be entered manually.
3. Make several copies of your data sheet(s) and data disk(s) after the data are recorded. Keep at least one copy in a safe place apart from the others.

As computers become smaller and more powerful, optical scanning-in of data is replacing direct keyboard entry of data. The same principles of data organization and formatting that have been used with the keyboard entry can be used with scanned entry.

Subject ID No.	Gender	Age	Education	BI	SR	VA	SEI	MD
001	2	1	3	6	28	08	3	06
002	1	3	2	5	06	12	5	24
003	1	2	4	7	33	09	8	08
004	2	2	1	4	14	14	7	19
Etc.	Etc.	Etc.	Etc.	Etc.	Etc.	Etc.	Etc.	Etc.

Code for variables: Gender 1 = female; 2 = male

Age: 1 = under 20   4 = 40 – 49
       2 = 20 – 29   5 = 50 – 59
       3 = 30 – 39   6 = 60 and over

Education: 1 = high school graduate   BI = Boredom Index
            2 = some college, but not graduate   SR = Spatial Relations
            3 = college graduate   VA = Visual Acuity
            4 = post-college graduate   SEI = Silence Endurance Index
                                          MD = Mechanical Dexterity

Figure 1: Example of a layout sheet for data on the STAT study

Gender of Subject
Age of Subject
Education of Subject

1. How long have you been using KISS?

    1 ☐ less than 5 years   2 ☐ more than 5 years

2. This questionnaire is being filled out by a(n)

    1 ☐ Earthling   3 ☐ Saturian

    2 ☐ Martian   4 ☐ Neptunian

3. Listed below are some patron services available to KISS travelers. We are interested in how often you use these services and how satisfied you were with them. Please circle one answer on the left and one answer on the right of each service listed.

I USE THIS   QUALITY IS

Very often	Occasionally	Seldom or never		Good	Fair	Poor	No opinion
1	2	3	Nutrient dispenser	1	2	3	4
1	2	3	Imagery simulator	1	2	3	4
1	2	3	Exerci-sor	1	2	3	4
1	2	3	Music-a-lator	1	2	3	4
1	2	3	Game simulator	1	2	3	4
1	2	3	Dialoguer	1	2	3	4
1	2	3	Insta-shower	1	2	3	4
1	2	3	Dream Analyzer	1	2	3	4

(continued next page)

4. Regarding the terminal or station you just left, what is your opinion of the following?

	Good	Fair	Poor	No opinion
Cleanliness	1	2	3	4
Overall station appearance	1	2	3	4
Moving sidewalk	1	2	3	4
Time spent at token booths	1	2	3	4
Time spent waiting for shuttle	1	2	3	4
Teleporters	1	2	3	4
Multi-lingual signs	1	2	3	4

5. What is your opinion of KISS capsules?

	Good	Fair	Poor	No opinion
Seating	1	2	3	4
Air conditioning	1	2	3	4
Heating	1	2	3	4
Cleanliness	1	2	3	4
Smoothness of ride	1	2	3	4
Noise of ride	1	2	3	4
Lighting	1	2	3	4
Doors	1	2	3	4
Station Announcements	1	2	3	4

(continued next page)

6. Over the last five years or so, do you feel each of the following has been improving, not changing, or getting worse?

	Getting better	Not changing	Getting worse	No opinion
Courtesy of KISS androids	1	2	3	4
Appearance of KISS robots	1	2	3	4
Adequacy of crowd control	1	2	3	4
Shuttle scheduling	1	2	3	4
KISS information service	1	2	3	4

7. Comments or suggestions _____

_____

_____

_____

_____

Figure 2: Example of a precoded questionnaire:

"Reactions to the KISS"

(Krazey Interplanetary Space Shuttle)

1) Study a statistics booklet; do exercises suggested by your instructor.

2) Cite examples when each of these statistics may be computed:
   a) Central tendency: mean, median, mode
   b) Variability: SD, Q, range
   c) Relative position: percentiles, z-scores
   d) Relationship: product-moment (r), rank-difference (R), biserial r, point-biserial r, contingency coefficient, phi coefficient.

3) A researcher sought an answer to this question: "Do earthwomen earn significantly higher scores on the Federated Galaxy Studies Test than Plutofemes?"
   a) State the research hypothesis.
   b) State the null hypothesis.
   c) How would you define and determine "significantly" higher scores?

4) The null hypothesis was rejected at the .01 level of significance. What does this mean?

5) In the t-test, how is sample size related to the t-value? What does it mean when we ascertain the statistical significance of our data?

6) Cite examples of studies which may require each of the following procedures:
   a) t-test for significance of the difference between independent (uncorrelated) means
   b) t-test for significance of the difference between correlated means
   c) analysis of variance (one-way)
   d) analysis of variance (two-way)
   e) analysis of covariance

#5: Measurement in Research

All descriptive and experimental research[1] studies involve some kind of measurement. By <u>measuring</u> we mean assigning a number or a symbol to an observation (e.g. score of 48 on a reading test, a value of 15 on an attitude scale, a temperature reading of 86 degrees, or a checkmark on a questionnaire). Two related terms are <u>testing</u> and <u>evaluating</u>. <u>Testing</u>, as it applies to people, is a systematic procedure for eliciting responses from one or more persons. For example, all students take the same reading test (under the same conditions) or all participants in an interview study respond to the same questions.

In comparison, <u>evaluating</u> denotes placing value judgments upon the outcomes of testing. For example, a test score of 72 is "good" (the student passes), or the test results suggest that the experiment was "successful," or the interview responses indicate that a certain political candidate is "very much liked." Evaluation is also thought of in broader terms than testing and measurement because it includes the use of qualitative assessment devices such as anecdotal records, logs, diaries, and biographical data forms. Thus, evaluation includes both qualitative and quantitative descriptions of behavior in addition to the value judgments concerning the desirability of that behavior.

In recent years, emphasis has been placed on describing evaluation in terns of how the various assessment devices are used. <u>Formative</u> evaluation is the monitoring of an ongoing program to provide feedback for its improvement. In educational programs, the feedback would be used to improve the teaching and learning – not to assign grades. <u>Summative</u> evaluation, on the other hand, would come at the end of the program or course of instruction and would be used to determine the extent to which the program was successful or the degree to which the student achieved in a course of study. Thus, the program would be retained, revised, or terminated; the student would be assigned a grade and either pass or fail.

However, in this chapter we shall treat measurement from the research point of view and discuss in some detail the concepts of validity, reliability and response set – concepts which are relevant to descriptive and experimental research.[2]

---

[1] Descriptive research will be discussed in Chapter #7, experimental research in Chapter #8.
[2] For more extensive discussions of these and related concepts, refer to APA (1988), Cronbach (1990), and Sax (1997).

By <u>validity</u> we mean the extent to which a research tool (such as a test, a questionnaire, or an interview guide) measures what it intends to measure. <u>Reliability</u> denotes the consistency of getting the same or similar responses (such as scores on a test, answers to a questionnaire, or replies in an interview). <u>Response set</u> is a consistent tendency to follow a certain pattern in responding to items in a test, a questionnaire, or an attitude scale.

Validity

The tools used in descriptive research are usually tests, questionnaires, interview guides, attitude scales, etc. These tools must be valid so that meaningful information can be gathered. With respect to experiments, it is imperative that the equipment and apparatus used by the experimental researcher are appropriate (that is, valid) for the task at hand.

We will now discuss the different types of validity with applications to the test, the questionnaire, and the attitude scale. The three major types of validity are <u>content, criterion-related</u>, and <u>construct</u>. (Occasionally, reference is also made to "face validity." This type of validity denotes the degree to which persons taking the test or responding to a questionnaire perceive it to be important. One should avoid instruments that appear to be trivial or demeaning, e.g., using childish words for older slow learners.)

Content Validity

As the name implies, here we are concerned with the content of our research tool – such as the test, questionnaire, or attitude scale. Since we cannot include an unlimited number of items in our test, questionnaire or attitude scale, we must select a limited number of items from a universe of items which could be included. Are the items included in the test related to the subject matter tested and to the stated objectives of a course of study or program? Are the kinds and numbers of items comprising the test reflecting the emphasis placed in a course or a program? Are the items representative of the universe of items? These are questions of professional judgment and are, therefore, <u>non-statistical</u> in nature.

After the objectives of a course of study or a program have been established, the test constructor writes a "test blueprint." This test blueprint is a two-way chart which relates specific objectives to specific content areas. The test constructor also lists the number of items which are designed to asses a specific objective within a specific content area. Examples of two kinds of test blueprints may be found on pages 52 and 53. The blueprint of the Federated Galaxy Studies Test (page 52) shows how the 100 items are distributed over the specific objectives and content areas. The test constructor indicates which <u>specific</u> test items are designed to measure which specific objective/content area. The blueprint of the Unit Test in Bookkeeping (page 53) tells us something about the content of the items as well as their distribution.

As a researcher contemplating the use of a certain test, you should take a hard look at the test and its manual to determine whether it is "valid" for your purpose; that is, you should examine the test blueprint as well as the test items themselves. For instance, if you wish to assess the effectiveness of a remedial reading program, you should examine very carefully the content validity of potentially useful criterion tests, such as the Spache Diagnostic Reading Scales or perhaps the Metropolitan Achievement Test. That is, are the test items measuring the program objectives?

The notion of a "test blueprint" also applies to the questionnaire. Obviously, first we have to set down the objectives of our survey and spell out the specific information which we are seeking. Then we are ready to write questionnaire items which are based on our objectives and thus geared to yield us the information sought. If the items really do correlate with the objectives and information sought, then our questionnaire has content validity. An example of a blueprint of a questionnaire may be found on page 52. Pre-testing of specific items is also recommended to determine your respondent's age by the item "Age ____," then the answer is ambiguous. Was the age recorded to the nearest birthday or to the next birthday? It would be better to list this item as "Date of Birth _____."

The notion of "good sampling from a universe of items," which is the basis for content validity, applies equally to an attitude scale such as racial attitudes. Does the scale touch all or most bases of this complex construct called "racial attitudes?" Are most areas of interracial encounters represented in the scale? Only a rational examination of the scale will give you the answers. Thus content validity is also sometimes referred to as <u>logical</u> validity.

Criterion-Related Validity: Concurrent and Predictive

While content validity embraces rational, logical, or judgmental considerations, criterion-related validity is established empirically (that is, <u>statistically</u>). The key to this type of validity is the <u>criterion</u> or the <u>criteria</u> (that is, a standard against which test scores or responses to a questionnaire or attitude scale can be assessed). This assessment or comparison is made by computing a correlation coefficient[3] between the scores on the to-be-validated research tool and the scores or responses on a criterion measure. For instance, if a researcher wishes to validate statistically a newly created intelligence test, scores of 100 people obtained on this test may be correlated with scores obtained by the same people on a reputable, very well-established intelligence test such as the Wechsler Adult Intelligence Scale (WAIS). In this case the researcher regards the WAIS as the acceptable criterion. The criterion measure need not be a test. The criterion measure could be behavior – in this case, "intelligent" behavior as judged by a number of trained observers. The more complex the behavior we are assessing, the more difficult it is to find an adequate criterion or criteria.

The comparison between the scores on the to-be-validated test and the criterion test could be made at about the same time or after a short time interval. This is known as concurrent validity. That is, the group of 100 people could be tested with the new, to-be-validated intelligence test today and be given the WAIS during the following week or two.

If a much longer time interval exists between the two test situations or the two assessment situations, then we are getting at predictive validity. For example, how valid is the SAT? Well, valid for what? To predict success in college. The SAT is our predictor test, given in high school, and "success in college" is our criterion variable, to be assessed two or more years later. We say that "success in college" is a criterion variable; it is not the criterion itself. What is the criterion or what are the criteria for "success in college?" Two common criteria are the grade point average (GPA) and graduation from college. If the SAT correlates highly with one or more of these criteria, then it is valid; that is, the SAT does predict "success in college" and can thus be an aid to guidance counselors.

Construct Validity

Constructs are any of the many psychological traits or characteristics such as anxiety, motivation, insecurity, self concept, introversion, intelligence, critical thinking and study skills. These constructs are not directly observable, but must be inferred on the basis of overt behavior. We cannot see "anxiety" but we can predict how people with varying degrees of anxiety will behave. The construct validity of a test denotes the extent to which it measures a

---

[3] The computation of correlation coefficients is presented in most statistics textbooks. For instance, you may refer to A practical guide to statistics for research and Measurement (Lang). Also, on page 55 you will find examples of the calculation of reliability correlation coefficients. The same procedure (formula) is used for getting a validity or reliability correlation coefficient. The procedure is the same; only the application differs.

theoretical construct or trait. While construct validity is concerned with a broad range of psychological traits, it is especially important in personality tests. It is used when one wishes to test a theory or to test predictions based on theory. For instance, someone has developed a paper and pencil test which purports to measure test anxiety. According to a certain theory of anxiety, perception is impaired and thinking processes are interfered with when a person is extremely anxious. A group of people similar in intelligence and knowledge of economics are given the Gesundheit Inventory of Text Anxiety and a test in economics. If the very high scorers on the test anxiety get low scores on the economics test, as predicted by one theory of anxiety, then the test is presumed to reflect a fair degree of "construct validity." In a similar vein, tests which claim to measure constructs like motivation or introversion can be validated by studying the behavior of people as predicted by psychological theories. If "loners" score highly on a test of introversion (i.e. the higher the score, the more introverted) while "joiners" score very low, then presumably the introversion test does seem to measure the construct "introversion" quite well.

Unlike content and criterion-related validity, construct validity is controversial, perhaps because it is somewhat nebulous. One can calculate coefficients of concurrent and predictive validity; however, there is no such thing as a coefficient of construct validity. Construct validity is investigated empirically and logically in a variety of ways, including the methods of content and criterion-related validity. "Evidence of construct validity is not found in a single study; rather, judgments on construct validity are based upon an accumulation of research results" (APA, 1988, p. 30)

The validity of the data is also an important concern in qualitative research. Usually, a researcher doing qualitative research collects data via different methods and uses different sources to ascertain her data's validity. For example, a researcher conducts an open-ended interview with a company executive to ascertain her perception of her effectiveness in running her department. To check on the plausibility of the collected interview data, the researcher may also interview fellow-employees. She may also check on the executive's effectiveness by noting criteria such as the productivity of the organization, attendance records and employee turnover rate.

Reliability

Reliability, another important attribute of a research tool, refers to the consistency of getting the same or similar responses – such as   scores on a test, answers to a questionnaire, or replies in an interview. Would you be satisfied with a car which gives you unreliable service – that is, starts inconsistently or stalls at most inconvenient times? Why should we use a research tool which is unreliable or less reliable than it could be? Do we get consistent, reliable responses to a survey instrument? Is the equipment used in an experiment reliable? Do we get accurate readings?

The reader should note that reliability is asking: to what extent does the instrument agree with itself; while validity asks: to what extent does the instrument accomplish its objectives? Thus, both characteristics are alike in that most types of validity and reliability require a comparison of two groups of data using a correlation technique. However, they are different in that reliability requires the instrument to be compared with itself or some form of itself while validity requires the comparison to be made with an outside or independent criterion.

Reliability may be considered in two respects: <u>one</u>, the accuracy of the score of one person; the <u>other</u>, the consistency of scores of a group of people.

Accuracy of One Person's Score

The person's score obtained on a test or in a bowling game is not the person's true score. The <u>true</u> score contains no errors of measurement (that is, it is a perfectly reliable score). The <u>obtained</u> score, on the other hand, does contain errors of measurement, reflecting changes within the person as well as within the testing conditions. We can estimate the amount of measurement error inherent in the obtained score and thus have some notion of how accurately we may know the person's true score. This estimate is given to us by the Standard Error of Measurement.

For example, suppose Mary obtains a score of 105 on the MW Intelligence Test. Let us assume that for this test the Standard Error of Measurement has been calculated to be 5.0. We know that Mary's "obtained score" is 105 but this is most likely not her "true score." However, based on certain psychometric calculations, we can say that if Mary were to take a large number of comparable tests (not the same tests), on 2/3 of these tests, her "true score," though unknown to us, would fall between 100 and 110, i.e. her "obtained score" of 105 ± 5.0 (the standard error of measurement). Another example. Helen obtained a score of 80 on a math test which has an error of measurement of 4.0. We do not know Helen's "true score." However, we know that if she were to take a large number of comparable tests, on 2/3 of the these tests her "true score" would fall between 76 and 84, i.e. her "obtained score" of 80 ± 4.0

(the standard error of measurement). In the case of Mary and Helen, as well as in all other cases, knowing the standard error of measurement should alert us to the fact that "obtained scores" containing errors of measurement, are not "true scores." Therefore, all obtained scores must be interpreted cautiously.

Listed below is a table of standard errors of measurement for given values of reliability coefficients and standard deviations[4].

SD	Reliability Coefficient					
	.95	.90	.85	.80	.75	.70
30	6.7	9.5	11.6	13.4	15.0	16.4
28	6.3	8.9	10.8	12.5	14.0	15.3
26	5.8	8.2	10.1	11.6	13.0	14.2
24	5.4	7.6	9.3	10.7	12.0	13.1
22	4.9	7.0	8.5	9.8	11.0	12.0
20	4.5	6.3	7.7	8.9	10.0	11.0
18	4.0	5.7	7.0	8.0	9.0	9.9
16	3.6	5.1	6.2	7.2	8.0	8.8
14	3.1	4.4	5.4	6.3	7.0	7.7
12	2.7	3.8	4.6	5.4	6.0	6.6
10	2.2	3.2	3.9	4.5	5.0	5.5
8	1.8	2.5	3.1	3.6	4.0	4.4
6	1.3	1.9	2.3	2.7	3.0	3.3
4	.9	1.3	1.5	1.8	2.0	2.2
2	.4	.6	.8	.9	1.0	1.1

Now ponder these questions:

(1) What is a person's <u>true</u> score on a test?

(2) How would we get this true score?

(3) Which factors contribute to the inaccuracy, thus unreliability, of a person's <u>observed</u> score?

(4) What is the Standard Error of Measurement?

(5) How is it interpreted?

---

[4] Test Service Bulletin #50 (The Psychological Corporation)

<u>Consistency of Scores of a Group of People</u>

Here we are concerned with the reliability (that is, the consistency) of scores or answers of a group of people. The three kinds of reliability relevant to a group of scores are: (1) internal consistency; (2) equivalence; and (3) stability.

<u>Internal consistency</u> deals with reliability derived from the administration of a <u>single</u> test or a <u>single</u> questionnaire or a <u>single</u> interview.

<u>Equivalence</u> presupposes the existence of two parallel (that is, equivalent) test forms or two versions of a questionnaire. Equivalent test forms or questionnaires are administered to a group of people at about the same time or with very little time lapse.

<u>Stability</u> data are based upon either the administration of the <u>same</u> test after a substantial time lapse or upon the administration of one test version <u>here</u> and <u>now</u> and an equivalent test version <u>after</u> a substantial time interval.

Evidence for all three types of reliability are indicated by a <u>reliability correlation coefficient</u>. This reliability correlation coefficient is determined by a number of different procedures, such as rank-difference of product-moment.

Look at the chart (page 54) which shows the type of consistency indicated by each method for estimating reliability. You will note that each method for estimating reliability provides different information concerning the consistency of test results. It is clear that most methods are concerned with only two types of consistency sought in test results. Internal consistency (split-half and Kuder – Richardson) takes into account the consistency of testing procedures and the consistency of results based on different samples of items. This method does not reflect constancy of pupil characteristics since only one test is given at one time. <u>Equivalence</u> and <u>test-retest stability</u> also reflect only two types of consistency. Only <u>equivalent forms stability</u> takes into account all three types of consistency. Therefore, this method is generally regarded as the most useful estimate of test reliability. Higher reliability correlation coefficients obtained via <u>internal consistency</u> are not as impressive as lower ones obtained via <u>stability (equivalent forms with time interval)</u>.

An analogy with your car may bring home this point.

We all like high gas mileage, just like a high correlation coefficient is most desirable. But is 40 miles per gallon impressive and realistic when this was obtained by a professional driver on an open highway and on a sunny day? The car driven by you in regular traffic and under varying weather conditions may only give you 20 miles per gallon, but this result is more realistic and more meaningful.

Methods of Determining Reliability Correlation Coefficients

Reliability correlation coefficients for the different methods of estimating reliability are obtained as follows[5]:

Internal Consistency

(a) split half: A single test is divided into two equal halves, the odd and even items. Two scores are obtained for each person – one based on the even test items, the other based on the odd test items. A correlation coefficient is computed between the two scores of the group of persons tested. This correlation coefficient is obtained by correlating the scores of two half-tests. Generally, the longer the test, the more reliable it is. Since the correlation obtained is only based on half of the test, a correction must by applied in order to get the reliability of the entire test. The Spearman – Brown formula is used for that purpose.

(b) Kuder – Richardson: KR formula #21 is listed on page 54. Scores based on the total test are used. For the group of persons tested, the mean and standard deviation (SD) have to be computed. The appropriate values are substituted into the formula and the KR estimate of reliability is obtained.

Equivalence

A group is tested with equivalent (parallel) forms of a test. A correlation coefficient is computed between the scores of the two tests.

Stability

A group is either (a) re-tested, with or without some time interval (with the same test); or (b) administered, after some time interval, an equivalent form of the test. The scores derived from the two administrations are correlated.

---

[5] Examples of the calculation of reliability correlation coefficients are shown on page 54.

Reliability of Questionnaire and Interview Responses

While all three types of reliability are also applicable to questionnaire and interview responses, <u>internal consistency</u> is most feasible. A researcher is delighted to obtain respondents' cooperation to fill out <u>one</u> questionnaire or to respond to <u>one</u> interview, but cannot really expect such cooperation when two questionnaires or interviews are involved.

Internal consistency of questionnaire and interview responses can be ascertained by asking for the same item of information in two or three slightly different ways. A reliable (consistent) respondent should reply in the same way. Also, one can ask for some data which can be easily verified, thus checking up on the respondent. For example, if you ask for the approximate population of the hometown and you are given a way–off figure, then you may well question the reliability of other bits of information which you have received.

Response Set

When we administer an attitude scale of a personality inventory, we are interested in obtaining individual perceptions on reactions. But there are styles of responding, called <u>response set</u>, which may interfere with our getting useable data. Examples of such subject response sets include avoiding extreme response options, giving socially expected responses, faking, offering very few of very many responses, etc. A discussion of observer of rater response sets is found on pages 101 + 102. Let us illustrate one subject response set and how to cope with it. Suppose you have a 25-item attitude scale, with each item responded to in terms of "strongly agree" or "agree" or "uncertain" or "disagree" or "strongly disagree." Timid or noncommittal respondents could check the "uncertain" category for each item. They are avoiding the extreme response options and the moderate options as well. These kinds of responses are not really usable. You must do something to force the respondent's hand. You can do that by instructing him/her to select three items with which he/she "strongly disagrees." Then he/she is to select five items with which he/she "agrees" and five with which he/she "disagrees." The remaining nine items fall into the "uncertain" category. In so doing, you are forcing the respondent to reveal his/her strong feelings pro or con on a certain issue. Several personality tests or inventories have built-in safeguards against response sets, such as faking or giving socially acceptable responses.

The keypoint is that standardized tests, questionnaires, attitude scales, and interviews are self-report type techniques and thus may elicit lopsided or distorted responses due to response set. This phenomenon also occurs in observational techniques. That is, observers and raters are also subject to such response sets as the "halo effect," "error of central tendency," and the "generosity error." Chapter #9 presents a more detailed treatment of these response sets[6].

A researcher who intends to develop an attitude scale or a personality inventory should learn more about response sets and means of identifying and controlling them.

---

[6] The Minnesota Multiphasic Personality Inventory (MMPI) and the Edwards Personal Preference Schedule (EPPS) have attempted to identify and control certain response sets. Cronbach (1990) discusses these two tests as well as response sets.

Blueprint of a Federated Galaxy Studies Test

Objectives	% of Time	C o n t e n t				
		Saturn	Pluto	Mars	Venus	Total
Recognizes important persons and their contribution to the galaxy	24	4	9	6	5	24
Knows major natural and synthetic resources	17	6	4	3	4	17
Understands strengths and weaknesses in political organizations	20	3	10	5	2	20
Evaluates significance of historical events	22	5	7	6	4	22
Assesses significance of cultural contributions to Earth	17	4	5	5	3	17
TOTAL	100	22	35	25	18	100

Blueprint of a Questionnaire: Follow-Up Study of Graduates of Galaxy II University, Department of Earth Studies

Information Sought	Questionnaire Section/Items
Identifying data (name, address, telephone number, etc.)	I: 1-5
Career goals	II: 1-9
Evaluation of specific courses	III: 1-31
Evaluation of specific instructional techniques	IV: 1-15
Major strengths of M.A. program	V
Major weaknesses of M.A. program	VI
Suggestions for improvement	VII

Blueprint of a Unit Test in Bookkeeping I[1]

CONTENT AREAS

Objectives	Check & Check Stub	Deposit Slip	Bank Reconciliation	Total
Recognizes terms, vocabulary, and forms	Check; Payee Check stub; Drawer Balance carried forward (5 items)	Drawn Deposit slip Cash ABA number (4 items)	Bank balance Outstanding checks Bank statement Deposit in transit Service charge Reconciliation (6 items)	15
Identifies specific facts	Place specific information is put on check and stub Bring balance forward on stub (4 items)	Difference between cash & checks Placement on deposit slip (3 items)	Outstanding checks & deposits Set up reconciliation (5 items)	12
Applies principles, concepts, and generalizations	Stub information, addition, subtraction completing check (5 items)	Listing checks and numbers (3 items)	Debits and credits pertaining to service charge, outstanding checks and deposits (5 items)	13
Recalls principles and concepts to apply to own experiences	Items left off sample check (3 items)	Using deposit slip (2 items)	Reasons why bank statement does not agree with checkbook (5 items)	10
Total	17	12	21	50

[1]Prepared by Mrs. Anna Vandermark in ELRS: 578.

Type of Consistency Indicated by Each Of the Methods for Estimating Reliability

| Estimating Method of Reliability | TYPE OF CONSISTENCY | | | Procedure |
	Consistency Of Testing Procedure	Consistency Of Pupil Characteristics	Consistency Over Different Sample of Items	
INTERNAL CONSISTENCY				
Split-half	*		*	Give test once. Score two equivalent halves (odd-even). Find r and correct with Spearman-Brown Prophesy Formula.
Kuder-Richardson	*		*	Give test once. Score test and apply KR Formula #21.
EQUIVALENCE	*		*	Give <u>two</u> <u>forms</u> of test to same group without time interval
STABILITY				Give <u>same</u> test twice to same group
Test-retest (immediate)	*			…without time interval…
Test-retest (time interval)	*	*		…with time interval…
				between the two test administrations.
Equivalent Forms	*	*	*	Give <u>two</u> <u>forms</u> of test to same group <u>with</u> time interval between the two test administrations.

<u>Spearman-Brown Formula</u>:

$$r = \frac{2r_{\frac{1}{2}}}{1 + r_{\frac{1}{2}}} \qquad r = \text{Reliability of the full test} \qquad r_{\frac{1}{2}} = \text{Reliability of the two half tests}$$

<u>Kuder-Richardson Formula No. 21</u>:

$r_{KR} =$ Estimate of reliability based on Kuder-Richardson $= \dfrac{n}{n-1}\left[1 - \left(\dfrac{Mean\left(1 - \dfrac{Mean}{n}\right)}{SD^2}\right)\right]$

$n =$ Number of items in the test $= \dfrac{75}{74}\left[1 - \left(\dfrac{50\left(1 - \dfrac{50}{75}\right)}{25}\right)\right] = 0.34$

(Example: n = 75, Mean = 50, SD = 5)

54

Calculation of Reliability Correlation Coefficients

Example: Internal consistency (split-half)

Student	Total Test	Odd Items	Even Items	Rank (odd)	Rank (even)	D	D²
A	40	22	18	2	5	3	9
B	41	20	21	4	2	2	4
C	31	17	14	7	10	3	9
D	28	13	15	10	9	1	1
E	40	21	19	3	4	1	1
F	34	18	16	6	7.5	1.5	2.25
G	39	19	20	5	3	2	4
H	45	23	22	1	1	-	-
I	32	16	16	8	7.5	1.5	2.25
J	32	15	17	9	6	3	9

$$\sum = 41.5$$

$$R = 1 - \left[\frac{6\sum D^2}{N(N^2-1)} \right]$$

$$= 1 - \left[\frac{6(41.5)}{10(99)} \right]$$

$$= 0.75$$

Spearman-Brown Formula

$$r = \frac{2r_{1/2}}{1 + r_{1/2}}$$

$$= \frac{2(0.75)}{1 + 0.75}$$

$$= \frac{1.50}{1.75} = 0.86$$

Example: Equivalence and Stability

Student	X	Y	Rank x	Rank y	D	D²
A	45	50	3	1	2	4
B	47	37	2	5	3	9
C	36	32	6	7	1	1
D	28	25	10	10	-	-
E	40	44	4	3	1	1
F	30	35	9	6	3	9
G	39	38	5	4	1	1
H	50	47	1	2	1	1
I	33	30	7	8	1	1
J	32	27	8	9	1	1

$$\sum = 28$$

$$R = 1 - \left[\frac{6\sum D^2}{N(N^2-1)} \right]$$

$$= 1 - \left[\frac{6(28)}{10(99)} \right] = 0.83$$

If Equivalence: X and Y are two forms of the test administered in close succession

If Stability (test-retest): X and Y are the same test, with time interval between the two administrations

If Stability (parallel forms): X and Y are two forms of the test, with time interval between the two administrations

1. Give examples of questionnaire items which seem to be ambiguous and thus may give invalid information. How could you establish the content validity of this questionnaire?

2. How could you validate (statistically) a racial attitude scale? ...a self-concept scale?

3. For which kinds of tests, questionnaires, interview guides, or attitude scales would predictive validity be most desirable?

4. What is the Standard Error of Measurement and how is it applied?

5. How could you ascertain the reliability of responses to questionnaires and interviews? Which method(s) would you use? How would you go about doing it?

6. Can a test be reliable but not valid? Can it be valid but not reliable?

7. What could you do to minimize the tendency to give socially expected answers rather than ones which reflect a person's true feelings?

#6: Types of Research: Historical, Documentary, Bibliographical and Construction

Various types of research exist and there are different ways of categorizing them. One may distinguish between quantitative and qualitative research. Quantitative research uses primarily statistical tools, whereas Qualitative research is primarily impressionistic and anecdotal. Marshall and Rossman (1989) and Strauss and Corbin (1990) are excellent sources for those who wish to embark on a qualitative research study.

There exists no distinct boundary line between quantitative and qualitative research. Both approaches are often used in combination. For instance, a researcher intends to conduct a case study (see Chapter #7) on an applicant for the position of ambassador to the Galaxy 23.6. The researcher may record impressionistic, phenomenological and anecdotal material (qualitative data) via an open-ended interview. She may also collect quantitative data, such as scores on achievement and personality tests, frequency and duration of illnesses, if any, as well as data elicited via numerical rating scales filled out by persons who know the applicant.

We have elected to categorize research as essentially either historical, descriptive or experimental in nature. Generally speaking, historical research … deals with the past through an analysis of remains and documents (i.e. "what was"); descriptive research deals with the present through an analysis of data gathered by questionnaire, interview, or observation (i.e. "what is now"); and experimental research is directed toward the future (i.e. "what will be or will occur under certain carefully controlled conditions"). It is possible and sometimes necessary to use all three types in solving problems. However, especially for the beginning researcher, it is best to keep one's project within bounds of only one of these categories.

In this chapter we will expand the notion of the historical category described above. We will discuss and make distinctions among four types of research projects: historical, documentary, bibliographical and construction. These possess many common characteristics. Some experts use the term "qualitative" to describe this family of research projects.

57

One purpose of this chapter is to emphasize the importance of the many studies done in history, anthropology[1] and the humanities that are basically verbal in data source and analysis.

This chapter is organized as follows: (1) definitions and examples of historical, documentary, bibliographical and construction research; (2) defining the problem and gathering the data; (3) criticism of sources; (4) writing the review of literature; and (5) writing the procedures section.

Definitions and Examples of Historical, Documentary, Bibliographical and Construction Research

These types of research are similar to other types of research in that they seek to solve problems in an objective and systematic way. They differ from descriptive and experimental research in that the historical researcher uses data which already exist in contrast to generating them via a questionnaire or a test as in descriptive research. This lack of data control is somewhat compensated for by the techniques of external and internal criticism discussed below.

People who are not too experienced with this type of research may equate it with writing a term paper or doing "library research," since most students entering an advanced degree program have already written many such papers during their school careers. One important question to keep in mind while reading this chapter is: What are the distinctive features of these types of research projects that make them more than just term papers?

Traditionally, historical research has been qualitative (non-statistical). However, in recent years more quantitative (statistical) approaches have been used. Examples of the latter are studies of readability of textbooks (applying one or more formulas of reading difficulty) and analysis of voting records of Democratic and Republican legislators. Many of the quantitative methods that have been developed are applications of content analysis.[2]

---

[1] See pages 95 or a brief discussion of ethnographic techniques used in anthropology as another category of qualitative research.
[2] See pages 78 & 79 for a discussion of this method.

Historical Research

This type of inquiry is often defined as the writing of an integrated narrative about some aspect of the past based on a critical analysis and synthesis of sources. Key words here are "integrated narrative" (which means more than quoting and simple reporting); "critical" (which refers to the use of principles of criticism); and "synthesis" (which implies the generation of tentative new knowledge within the limits of the sources and techniques available). In addition, the basic ordering element in history is time. That is, the historical method seeks to assess meaning over some significant period of time.

Some experts attempt to show the inter-relationships of history to science and social fields such as economics, sociology, literature, and psychology. History is viewed by them as an inclusive or mediating type of discipline which links various fields. In addition, through history one can develop a background perspective and insight into a person, problem, event, or institution not obtainable through other types of research. This is why all types of research have their historical component – namely, the review of literature section of the research project. However, in experimental or statistical research, historical methodology is not used to solve the basic problems of the researcher. In historical research, which is most often concerned with qualitative results, the historical methodology (i.e. the review and analysis of the literature) does generate the answers. Thus, in addition to being a mediating discipline and developing perspective, historical research can also be used to solve problems in the sciences, humanities, and education. For an excellent basic historical research methods book, see Gottschalk (1969).

One interesting branch of historical research is the study of family history and the related techniques of doing genealogy and oral history. Family history has been popularized by the success of Alex Haley's television series <u>Roots</u>, which helped demonstrate that every family has an oral history worth exploring.

Studying family history is much more than a self-serving exercise. By tracing our family's past, we learn to appreciate what it meant just to live and travel. We observe prosperity and depression not from the point of view of the leaders, but from the vantage point of the people who triumphed or suffered. We come to understand both the continuities of existence and how the passage of time has brought about change. We develop a relationship with past generations and eventually begin to realize that we are part of the ongoing movement of humanity. We come to better understand ourselves.

The best way to begin family history is with your own immediate family, especially grandparents and great-grandparents. Basic sources – in addition to taping interviews with your oldest living relatives – are the Bibles, wills, letters, deeds, marriage and death certificates, and the census records.

Fundamental to any type of research are the basic data-gathering questions that should be answered. For doing family research, some of the following types are suggested: (1) questions regarding birth, death, education, marriage, occupation, etc.; (2) questions regarding political, community, and family life; and (3) questions regarding social, economic, and religious identities and influences. See Appendix E for a sample of a working pedigree or heritage chart which is used to record some of this basic information.

In order to organize, synthesize, and interpret the data gathered, some of the following questions may be helpful: (1) How can we best describe and compare the life and times of our ancestors through various historical periods? (2) Who broke the cultural chain in your family (the person who first immigrated, the person who first moved off the farm, etc.) Who were other influential people, family and non-family? (3) What factors caused the migration and the other important events? How many significant events were there (positive or negative) stemming from economic, religious, political, or social forces? (4) What is there in this family history that explains how you came to your present location and position in life? An excellent source which stresses the educational aspects of family history and is also a resource for detailed research techniques and sources is Watts and Davis (1983).

Closely related to family history is oral history, which is a method of collecting historical information. Generally, it consists of well-planed tape-recorded interviews with participants and witnesses of historical events. The interviews are primary sources. Oral history is particularly important because with the passage of time, participants and witnesses die or their memories fade; lacking their personal record, we are left with a historical narrative based on secondary or even more remote sources. Its use in developing local and family history should be obvious.[3] However, it is also useful in a larger sense.

One of the most traumatic events in human history took place in the 1930's and 1940's when, during the Nazi regime in Germany, millions of people, particularly Jews, were tortured and killed. Toward the end of World War II, the allied armies liberated the survivors of the concentration camps and uncovered the details of the incredible atrocities that had been committed. Now referred to as the Holocaust, its survivors are being interviewed so that their experiences can be recorded before these witnesses to man's inhumanity to a man die out. In this instance, oral history serves as an educational technique to teach future generations about the horrible consequences of rampant racism.

Experts in the methods of research also devote time to the question of whether history is a science or humanity. Among all the pros and cons there appears to be general agreement that, while historians' principles of criticism and techniques of analysis and synthesis meet the standards of objectivity used in scientific methodology, history (unlike science) is not a discipline of direct observation, experimentation, and control. Finally, it might be said that the historian tends to look upon the rendering of the narrative as an artistic or literary work, while many statistical based researchers do not.

Some titles of this type of research are <u>Sex Education in Colonial Schools</u>, <u>Basic Objectives Employed in the Teaching of History in German Schools Since 1900</u>, <u>A Retrospective Analysis of Success or Failure of Special School District Levies in Essex County</u>, <u>A History of Montclair State University</u>, <u>The Contribution of William B. Stapp to Environmental Education</u>, and <u>An Account of the Life and Times of the Wood-Meier Families of Lebanon County PA.</u>

Documentary Research

There is often only a fine line of distinction to be made between this type of research and historical research. In some studies, the two approaches are combined into one category and called <u>historical-documentary</u> method. However, documentary research (when

---

[3] Several universities throughout our country serve as centers for the collection of oral history. For example, at the Oral History Center at Columbia University, remarks of important persons who might not write memories are recorded on tape. The Regional Oral History Office in the Bancroft Library at the University of California at Berkley is concerned with the collection and preservation of reminiscences of persons who have made important contributions to the development of the West.

used alone) usually excludes the use of historical remains and documents. Rather, it tends to emphasize contemporary sources and present-day issues. It can be thought of as cross-sectional, rather than longitudinal, where the data focus is on one point in time or a relatively short period of time. Whereas the task of the historian is to assess meaning through a reconstruction of the past, time may be an insignificant factor in any number of contemporary problems of interest to the researcher (e.g. the examination of current social issues such as civil rights, school prayers, equal employment opportunities, population problems and evaluation of various musical or literary works). Here, the important factors in analysis and synthesis are the search for commonalties, categories, influences, and trends, or (in the case of artistic works) such structural elements as plot, characterization, melody or rhythm.

Some titles of this type of research are <u>A Structural Analysis of Three Exemplary Novels</u> by Miquel de Umanuno, <u>An Analysis of the Master's Degree Programs in New Jersey State Colleges</u>, <u>An Evaluation of the Current Views of Senator Smith and Senator Moynihan Toward the Middle East.</u>

Bibliographical Research

Another related type of project is what some experts call a study of studies. This refers to the collection, analysis and synthesis of the significant empirical works done on a particular topic within a field (e.g. achievement motivation, group guidance, behavior modification, etc.). The purpose is to organize and structure those yet unsynthesized areas within fields of study and to identify topics still in need of further clarification. Although such research resembles a term paper, it is on a much higher level of comprehension and complexity. Thus, this research project is a study in its own right even though the basic data for it consist of other studies.

Another example of bibliographic research is meta-analysis. For this analysis the researcher combines the findings of several previous studies systematically and statistically. Mata-analysis is a form of research synthesis and integration. There exist several quantitative techniques which can be used to combine data from a variety of studies. Good examples of articles which use meta-analysis may be found in issues of the <u>Psychological Bulletin</u> and the <u>Review of Educational Research.</u> For a more detailed description of this technique, refer to Glass, McGraw and Smith (1981) and Rosenthal (1991)

Some titles of this type of research are <u>The Use of Ethnographic Techiques in Educational Research: An Analysis and Synthesis of the Methodological Literature</u>, <u>An Examination of the Expert Literature Concerning the Relationship of Overpopulation and Environmental Pollution</u>, and <u>Research on Curriculum Implementation: Its Meaning and Potential Determinants.</u>

Construction Research

Again, this type of research employs many of the techniques and skills used in doing historical-documentary research. However, here the focus is on producing or constructing a useful project. A continuous emphasis in research literature has been reference to the gap between theory and practice, between what is known and what is done, and the lack of educational materials to meet the needs of students and educators. Construction research tries to fill this gap. It should be emphasized that this type of research is not a mere complication of simplistic data like a listing of names and telephone numbers. Rather, the focus is on a scheme of analysis which will produce a different or unique structure and appropriate content. Thus, with this type of project, the student would propose to construct a new test, curriculum guide, pamphlet for parents, directory, or some other useful product.

Some titles of this type of research project are <u>A guide to Ecolog-logical Encounters in Rockland County, NY</u>, <u>A Directory of Non-Profit Vocational Guidance Programs for Non-College Adults in New Jersey</u>, and <u>A Departmental Achievement Test in U.S. History for Montclair High School.</u>

Defining the Problem

Usually the most worthwhile research projects are derived from the students' interests and needs. We hope a project will be found that is related to the students' everyday or future professional progress and will be helpful in solving a meaningful educational problem.

As with all types of research, a purpose or problem statement is absolutely necessary before proceeding with the formal gathering and analysis of sources. The first problem, then, is to find a problem! This may take considerable time in thinking, reading and discussion. But, sooner or later, a clear-cut problem statement must be derived so that analysis and synthesis can proceed in a systematic way.

Generally, one attempts to tell how and what he or she intends to do in a succinct paragraph. An example of a problem statement for a <u>historical</u> project might be: "The purpose of this project is to identify and categorize the sex education policy trends and factors influencing those trends in the Newark schools during the period 1900 – 1996 through a study of the official Board of Education records and publications." A more <u>documentary</u> type project, perhaps done in the political science field, might have the following statement: "The purpose of this research is to determine the positions of Senator Moynihan and Senator Smith on the Middle East by comparing and contrasting their statements as found in the current Congressional Record." A <u>construction</u> project might propose the following: "The purpose of this project is to construct a supplemental curriculum guide through an analysis of model guides and other expert sources to use in teaching eight grade arithmetic to gifted children." A <u>bibliographic</u> project might pose the following problem: "The purpose of this project is to analyze the current ethnographic research literature to identify the basic differences between it and conventional research, and to explain the rationale and techniques by which ethnographic research is conducted." Such problem statements may be altered as one gets deeper into the project due to lack of time, lack of sources, or other factors. However, the revised statement must retain its clarity of purpose and method.

Another helpful idea to consider at this point is a hierarchy of problem statements moving from the simple to the complex. Some experts note three levels: descriptive, analysis of factors, and hypothesis testing. At the first level, one identifies and describes the who, what, when and where facts. Thus, a descriptive level treatment of the history of one's school system would include such information as numbers and disposition of pupils, staff, buildings, and the like. At the second level, the study is more complex because the researcher promises to identify and explain those institutions, conditions, events, persons, and elements that were factors in establishing structure, influence, and trends. Finally, one moves farthest from simple description when one seeks to test hypotheses and show cause and effect.

At this point the reader is directed to Gottschalk's concept of the interrogative hypothesis. Gottschalk suggests that in analyzing a document, it is more productive to approach it with a question or group of questions than with a declarative statement. A standard approach to historical-documentary analysis is to begin by using an overall idea or hypothesis (declarative statement) as a guide in order to prevent aimless gathering of isolated facts; this overall idea may later develop into a full-fledged declarative hypothesis.

Gottschalk, however, suggests it is more "scientific" to begin by raising specific questions rater than making statements. Such questions, asked before the evidence is in, are less committal than statements. They are free from the bias of a preconceived hypothesis and they aid in the problem of relevancy since it is obvious that only those sources which help answer the question are relevant. (For a more detailed discussion of these ideas, see Gottschalk, Kluckhohn, Andell, 1945)

The notion of a hierarchy of problem statements is important because it is directly related to the analysis and organization of data. It should be clear that each succeeding level of analysis requires a more complex approach as one moves toward showing cause-effect relationships.

Type of Data Sources

A discussion of references, library skills and sources was presented in Chapter #3. Several additional points need emphasis at this time.

The neophyte researcher should soon begin to realize that there is a vast array of sources available or at least existing such as physical remains (sites, human remains, machinery, etc.); orally transmitted materials, representative materials with symbols but not with true writings (inscriptions on clay, monuments, stamped coins, tapestries, etc.); handwritten materials (ancient manuscripts and scrolls, chronicles, biographies, diaries, letters, etc.); the whole range of printed matter; the whole range of audio-visual matter; and personal observation and interview.

A second point that needs emphasis is the distinction among preliminary sources, primary sources, and secondary sources. Preliminary sources are what some experts call the master keys to unlocking library information. These are the abstracts, indexes, bibliographies, encyclopedias and yearbooks which enable the researcher to locate the principle studies in one's area of interest. The students should be familiar with some of the following examples of preliminary sources: Education Index, Dissertation Abstracts, Psychological Abstracts and Encyclopedia of the Social Sciences.

Generally, research which is basically non-statistical draws upon two kinds of sources: primary and secondary. Primary sources are the original documents and remains, the first witness to the event, with only the mind of the observer coming between the original event and user of the source. Many of the sources listed previously in Good's classification are examples of primary sources. <u>Secondary</u> sources are the reports of a person who records the testimony of an actual witness of or participant in an event. This person was not on the scene but reports what the actual witness said or wrote. Thus, a secretary's notes of a meeting would be primary data while a reporter's newspaper account of the meeting based on the secretary's notes would be a secondary source. Secondary sources tend to be less worthwhile (however, many times this is all you have) because of the greater chance for error and bias as information is passed on from one person to another. The use of primary data tends to strengthen the integrity of the study and thus the quality of scholarship may be judged in part by what effort the student makes to obtain primary data. Finally, at times it is also the nature and purpose of the research problem which determines whether a particular source is primary or secondary. For example, a textbook is ordinarily a secondary source. But if one were making a study of the author's philosophy toward a subject, the textbook might then function as a primary source.

Criticism of Sources

The researcher has an obligation to determine the genuineness and truthfulness of the sources used. Over the years, a body of principles of criticism has developed which some experts have divided into two categories and labeled <u>external</u> and <u>internal</u> criticism. Some scholars use the term "historical science" when referring to this body of principles which aid the researcher in deriving verifiable evidence from sources.

<u>External</u> criticism gets at the authenticity of the document rather than at the meaning of its content. Thus it is concerned with the possibilities of forgeries, ghost writing, errors and completeness. The problem of establishing authenticity may involve tests of signature, language usage or physical and chemical tests. Carbon dating is one obvious example. Most students (unless they are doing a basically historical project) will not often encounter the need to determine the authenticity of the modern sources they usually use. There appears to be little reason to forge a school textbook or a new curriculum guide. However, there may be some limited concern about completeness, ghost writing and copying errors.

<u>Internal</u> criticism deals with the credibility of the source. Thus all may agree on who wrote it, but can it be believed and what does it mean? Experts have developed specific maxims or tests for credibility. Gottschalk (1969), for example, asserts that any source that passes all four of the following tests is credible evidence: (1) Was the primary witness able to tell the truth - this involves nearness, competence, degree of attention, etc.; (2) Was the

primary witness willing to tell the truth - this involves being an "interested witness," bias, literary style, etc.; (3) Was the primary witness accurately reported - this is a concern when secondary witnesses must be used; and (4) Is there independent corroboration – this requires the testimony of two or more reliable witnesses.

Again, it seems that unless the student is attempting a piece of historiography or a textual study in literature, it should not be necessary to subject the documentary sources to an exhaustive set of maxims of criticism. However, the fundamental task of the researcher is to get as close as possible to the truth. This idea cannot be overemphasized! The point is that we probably never find the "whole truth and nothing but the truth, " but we try to come as close as we can through a critical study of the best available sources. Our truth becomes a tentative kind of truth rather than absolute kind of truth. Tests of internal criticism direct the researcher's attention to the great difficulty in evaluating the impact of competence, motivation, bias and other factors on the sources used. For example, how do we evaluate the account of an acrimonious board of education meeting written by the superintendent in the absence of the secretary? Would the superintendent tend to present a one-sided point of view? Or consider the following two books dealing with a comparable period in history: Shirer's Rise and Fall of the Third Reich and Speer's Inside the Third Reich. Shirer was an American correspondent and historian; Speer was a Nazi war criminal and was a close intimate of Hitler. Consider the problems in determining the truthfulness of these two books.

Writing the Review of the Literature

Finally, it is important to understand that in doing non-statistical or qualitative research, the review of the literature is handled differently than in most statistical type projects. The reason for this difference is that in this case the literature reviewed is the source of data. In most statistical type projects, data are generated through questionnaires, tests or other instruments and the review of the literature provides only supporting and background data. In addition, the literature in non-statistical studies also may be less reliable and more difficult to find. This is because it tends to have a qualitative rather than a quantitative nature and may be located out of the mainstream of conventional sources.

Therefore, it is suggested that in the introduction to the review of literature, the student indicate at least two things: (1) Tell briefly what libraries and other retrieval and depository systems were used; and (2) Tell how the sources were categorized.

In the body of the review, identify and describe briefly the sources you expect to use and why they were selected – what you hope to get from them. In statistical type projects, it is important to conclude with a critical summary. This is less important in historical-documentary research, for it tends to push the researcher toward an analysis and synthesis of sources and thus actually to begin carrying out the research itself.

Writing the Procedures Section for Non-Statistical Research

This last section will attempt to deal in general with the techniques of writing non-statistical research projects and in particular with writing the procedures section of the research proposal. See Appendix F for an example.

It is customary to begin the procedures section of the proposal with a short overview statement which briefly describes the purpose and method of the project. This allows the reader to skip directly to the procedures section and still read with understanding.

The second part of this section consists of an overview of sources and a consideration of the problems of criticism. Here the researcher presents a brief summary of sources used and directs the reader to see the review of the literature for detailed treatment. At this juncture, the principles of criticism are recognized and any potential problems with authenticity, completeness, credibility and the like are indicated.

The third part of the procedures section should be devoted to techniques of analysis and synthesis. However, one should not make this mistake of thinking that these steps are taken neatly one after the other, because the struggle for insight as one ties the data together starts almost from the beginning. Guiding questions in the synthesis process are: (1) What are my specific purposes; what questions am I answering and what hypothesis is guiding my research? (2) What is my level of complexity – descriptive narrative, analysis of trends, influences, relationships or hypothesis testing? (3) What are my organizational principles; is my project one which has a basic agreed-upon design like a curriculum guide, or does it require more original thinking? How will I use such methods of internal organization and classification as inductive and deductive presentation, cause-effect, comparison and contrast techniques, and such ordering elements as space and time?

Thus, it should be clear that it is not the data that structure the project, but rather the ideas, insights and skills of the researcher. Barzun and Graff (1992) insist that to be effective, a mass of words must have form. That form must meet the conflicting demands of

68

unity (one topic at a time) and chronology (a series of topics in order), while also holding the reader's attention. This requires coherence, which depends on the ability to pass from one paragraph, section and chapter to another. And this finally depends on one's skill and use of <u>transitions</u>. Much effort and practice is needed to develop these complex skills. The interested student is advised to study the detailed treatment found in such sources as Barzun and Graff (1992).

The final part of the procedures section contains the presentation of the tentative outline or table of contents. In one important way, this has been the goal of the researcher almost from the beginning and gradually emerges as the sources are criticized, analyzed and digested. The first attempt may be incomplete and ragged; however, it is useful as a guide in locating and recording necessary data or in omitting information that looks good but, in fact, contributes little to the overall objective. One is not bound by the first outline; for, as data gathering continues, new topics may be added, others refined or discarded, and order rearranged. That is, as the study progresses, the outline should be revised accordingly.

Exercises for Chapter #6

Part A

1. What is the significance of considering historical type research as being primarily qualitative rather than quantitative in database and technique?

2. How and where does historical perspective function in all types of research? How does the use of historical methodology differ when doing historical research as compared to statistical types of research?

3. Why is doing local and family history more than just a self-serving exercise?

4. What are the distinguishing features of historical, documentary, bibliographical, and construction research?

5. How is the level of the problem statement related to the procedures for carrying out the project?

6. Make the distinction among and give examples of preliminary, primary and secondary sources.

7. Identify and apply several principles of external and internal criticism. Use your text or specialized sources for examples. How will these principles of historical science be used in your project?

8. How and why is the review of the literature section treated differently in doing non-statistical research?

9. What are several specific guidelines the researcher can use to write the procedures section?

10. What are several specific guidelines the researcher can use to write the report? How does the skill of writing transitions play an important role?

Exercises for Chapter #6

Part B

1. Which kind of research problem could be most fruitfully attacked via the collection of new data?

2. Which kind of research problem could be most fruitfully attacked via the use of <u>existing</u> data?

3. How would you apply external criticism to a manuscript (or to a Chopin composition)?

4. In applying external and internal criticism to the books of Shirer and Speer as well as the "Hitler Diaries," what are you likely to find?

5. What could a historian do to minimize and counteract potential errors in conducting historical research?

6. What are the strengths and weaknesses of various types of qualitative research designs?

#7: Types of Research: Descriptive

Descriptive research deals with the present through the analysis of data gathered via various tools such as observation, questionnaire, interview, and test. Descriptive research describes and interprets <u>what</u> <u>is</u>. There exist many varieties of descriptive research studies. In this chapter we shall deal with five major ones: (1) status studies; (2) casual-comparative studies; (3) correlational studies; (4) case studies; and (5) content analysis.

Status Studies

As used in this context, status refers to a state or condition of affairs. Opinion polls, market research surveys, community surveys, follow-up studies, job analysis studies, and the census are examples of status studies. Examples of typical titles follow:

- Opinions of Earthlings with respect to admission of Venus into the Federated Galaxy

- Consumer acceptability of the Kleanaire Electric Car

- The need for a mental health center at Happytown

- Follow-up of graduates of the Galaxy Academy of Universal Learning

- Duties, responsibilities, and training required of world traffic advisors

- Human kindness as portrayed in 7-9 p.m. weekly TV shows of five major networks

- The state of the nation's dental health.

Polls and surveys usually involve only a sample or samples of people or specimens, while the census usually embraces a whole population of a universe of observations. The reasons for undertaking a status study are:

1. to obtain basic information, where none exists, on a problem, or to update information on a particular topic or condition

2. to correct misinformation

3. to collect data which are potentially useful for other research efforts.

Since these are all important reasons, it is not surprising that status studies are very popular.

The results of a status study, like those of any type of study, can be misused. For instance, a reader of a status study may feel that the description and interpretation of a phenomenon denotes its approval by the researcher. The researcher collects data on the "status quo," but neither approves nor disapproves of it. Suppose a researcher finds that many food products contain harmful chemicals and describes and interprets these observations. This does not mean, of course, that these observations represent a desirable state of affairs. However, a manufacturer of food products may rationalize continued production of his items on the basis of "everybody's doing it, so why not we?" Some status studies may yield upsetting and disturbing kinds of information. These potential consequences cannot be blamed on the researcher, only on the potential misusers.

Causal-Comparative Studies

This type of descriptive research, sometimes referred to as Ex Post Facto Design, attempts to seek answers to problems through an analysis of possible causal factors. Which factors seem to contribute to certain kinds of behavior, events, or conditions? We say "seem" to contribute because only experimental research[1] with its appropriate controls can ascertain cause-and-effect relationships. However, experiments cannot be conducted on phenomena which have already occurred (e.g. school vandalism) nor can we, ethically, manipulate certain variables (e.g. tooth decay, poor reading achievement) which inflict pain or hardship on people. The causal-comparative study represents an attempt to understand already manifested behavior, events or conditions by identifying possible causal factors which could explain why the behavior, events or conditions exist. Such a study does this by selecting two groups of subjects or sets of conditions which represent opposite poles of the particular situation or state to be studied.

Illustrative comparisons follow:

- two groups of teenagers (one with high, the other with low incidence of tooth decay)

---

[1] Experimental research will be discussed in Chapter #8.

- two inner city schools (one with mostly successful, the other with mostly unsuccessful readers)

- two drafting squads (one with good, the other with poor morale)

- two communities (one with much, the other with little school vandalism).

The questions in each instance are: Why is one group or community different from the other? Which factors differentiate between the two groups? To what extent can these factors be used and studied experimentally in order to determine cause-and-effect relationships?

We shall now present two specific examples of causal-comparative studies.

It is well known that heart disease is very common among urban American males. This disease is either absent or very uncommon among Andean Indians in Ecuador. Here we have two different, contrasted groups. Causal-comparative research would first focus on describing representative samples taken from these two groups with respect to lifestyle, diet, child rearing practices, environmental conditions, etc. This description may yield potential causal factors implicated in heart disease. Once these potential factors have been identified, they must be tested experimentally.

Suppose we wish to know what the factors are which distinguish "successful" from "unsuccessful" life insurance sellers with the ultimate purpose of selecting promising candidates. We first have to define operationally "successful" and "unsuccessful." Let's say "successful" sellers are those who sell $5,000,000 worth of life insurance per year (one extreme) and "unsuccessful" sellers are those who sell less than $500,000 per year (the other extreme). Then we select two groups from a specified sample—say, male, married, white, Catholic 30-39 year olds—and we compare them with respect to a number of variables which may have a bearing on their selling efforts. To what extent are these variables present or absent in each group? Perhaps we find that intelligence is a key distinguishing variable and that successful life insurance sellers are more intelligent—that is, have significantly higher WAIS I.Q.'s than unsuccessful sellers. Or, perhaps these good sellers know more about current events than do poor sellers. These are then potentially causal factors, helping us formulate hypotheses to be tested out in a subsequent study. That is, based on the emerging profile of "successful" life insurance sellers, we could select from a pool of job applicants only those who manifest these characteristics and determine in a longitudinal study whether this profile has predictive validity. The criterion is the amount of life insurance sold in a given year.

The value of a causal-comparative study can be enhanced if these guidelines are adhered to:

1. The variable or the characteristic which sets the groups or conditions apart must be operationally defined. That is, the criteria of "high" vs. "low" tooth decay, "good" vs. "poor" morale, etc., must be spelled out.

2. The contrasted groups or conditions must be equivalent in all respects except on the one variable or characteristic which sets them apart. That is, it would be wrong to use married men for the "successful" group of life insurance sellers and unmarried men for the "unsuccessful" group. Comparison groups (in this example) should comprise either married or unmarried men. In the projected study of school vandalism, both communities should be similar with respect to attributes such as location (urban or rural), size of school population, and socioeconomic status.

3. We must make certain that all or most relevant comparison factors are used. That is, we have to compare the two polar groups or conditions on a wide variety of factors assumed to be causal of the phenomenon to be studied. Omitted factors could be the ones which differentiate between two groups or conditions. Promising comparison factors in the study of life insurance sellers are intelligence, temperament, speech pattern, appearance, knowledge of the community, and the absence of annoying personal habits. However, this is probably not an all-inclusive list.

4. A causal-comparative study helps us identify factors which may cause a certain phenomenon (e.g. behavior, event, condition); however, only an experiment can yield us more definitive information.

Correlational Studies

A correlational study is one which, through the computation of a correlation coefficient, endeavors to discover a relationship (or association or link) between two or more variables. In Chapter #5 we have shown how correlation coefficients are used in ascertaining validity and reliability. Correlations may also be used to determine to what extent certain human characteristics have a unitary nature. For example, we may pose the question: "Is assertiveness a uni-dimensional trait?" By collecting data on people in different settings—on the job, in the home, among friends and colleagues, etc.—we can use the correlational method to see to what extent people are consistently assertive (i.e. do people act consistently?). Correlational studies are also used to make predictions. We may answer questions such as: "Are vocational interests related to job success?" or "Is compatibility related to marital bliss?"

Here are some other examples of correlationial studies, which can be used for predictions:

- Prices of stocks (New York Exchange) and interest rates (negative r)

- Gasoline cost and consumption (negative r)

- Food additives and hyperactivity in children (positive r)

- Severity of life changes and proneness to illness (positive r).

Davidson and Lang (1960) studied correlations among four variables: (1) children's perceptions of their teachers' feelings toward them; (2) self-perceptions; (3) academic achievement; and (4) classroom behavior. Significant positive correlations (associations or links) among all four variables were found. That is, children who perceived their teachers' feelings toward them as favorable tended to see themselves more favorably, achieved and behaved better in school.

When reviewing a correlatioinal study like this one, we must keep in mind that the finding of a significant correlation between two or more variables does not tell us that we have a cause and effect relationship. Variables may be correlated, but need not be causally related. In the study cited above, we cannot conclude that Variable (1) causes Variable (2), (2) causes (3), and (3) causes (4). We do know that these four variables are linked together, for whatever reasons, and that we can make certain predictions. For example, it is very likely that children with poor self images will underachieve and will misbehave; it is equally likely that underachieving, misbehaving children have poor self images. Even without knowing the specific reasons why these variables are correlated or what is causing each or all of these behaviors or conditions in a child, we can incorporate the information gained from this study into some course of action.

Correlational studies are very common and can be found in all kinds of professional journals, newspapers and magazines. They are very useful, particularly if the major caution is recalled: The finding of a significant correlation does not <u>necessarily</u> denote a clear-cut cause-and-effect relationship.

Case Studies

The case study can be categorized as a developmental, genetic, or clinical case study. It represents an <u>intensive</u> study of a phenomenon, using a variety of data sources and tools. The case study approach is <u>problem-oriented</u> and is applicable to an individual, a family, an institution, or a whole community. Examples for each kind of focus follow:

The individual: Why is Jane Doe a poor reader? ...or an underachiever? ...or a highly creative, productive member of her profession?

The family: Why is this a happy family? ...or an unhappy one?

The institution: How effective is this college in preparing educational leaders? Should this high school or that college be accredited?

The community: What is the quality of life in the community? How can specific problems (e.g. regarding drug use or racial tensions) be resolved?

The basic rationale for a case study is that there are processes and interactions such as aspects of social functioning and personality which cannot be studied effectively except as they interact and function within the entity itself. Thus, if we learn how these processes interact in one person or organization, we will know more about the processes as factors in themselves and perhaps apply these learnings to other similar type persons or organizations.

The case study approach calls for an <u>in-depth analysis</u> of the unit to be studied. Thus, it sets the stage for getting meaningful information. Its usefulness is diminished by the difficulty of getting <u>complete</u> and <u>dependable</u> data.

The case study can be a scientific endeavor if it is conducted in line with generally acceptable practices—i.e. through systematic collection of unbiased data, testing of hypotheses, and drawing valid conclusions. The results of the case study on a single unit (individual, family, institution, or community) may not be applicable to other units; however, they may provide clues for other studies or courses of action. For example, in studying the quality of life in Happytown we may find that this community has evolved effective means of coping with air pollution or drug abuse. This case study can help us when investigating and helping another community to resolve its problems.

You will find an example of an individual case study outline in Appendix G and one for a community in Appendix H.

Content Analysis

Content analysis may be generally defined as the systematic and objective use of techniques to quantify any form of communication. Types of communication range from the conventional documentary sources such as books and periodicals to recordings of observations, music, and pictures. Basically, this method of analysis consists of identifying and counting indicators of the variables in question.

Content analysis may be envisioned as one form of documentary analysis. It could be placed on a continuum ranging from those types which are most literary or historical to those involving counting and statistical analysis at the nominal and ordinal level. The less one uses quantification type techniques, the more one depends on the techniques derived from history and the humanities. Thus, this type of research may be seen as an intermediate process used to categorize verbal or behavioral data for purposes of classification, summarization, and tabulation.

Some of the purposes of this type of research identified by Best and Kahn (1993) are: (1) to describe prevailing practices and conditions; (2) to discover the relative importance of, or interest in, certain types of problems; (3) to discover the level of difficulty of a book or publication; (4) to evaluate bias or prejudice in a book or publication; (5) to analyze types of errors in students' work; and (6) to identify the literary style and beliefs of a writer.

For example, a content analysis of a social studies textbook could reveal the scope and sequence of the topics treated, the author's point of view toward the topics, the type of sources used by the author, the type of end-of-chapter activities, etc. Or the analysis could be an in-depth study of how minority groups were handled.

When embarking on a content analysis study, one has to: (1) decide what the unit will be which is to be analyzed; (2) develop a set of categories and indicators; and (3) develop a schema which guides the placement of observations into these categories. For example, in a study of commercials of children's TV programs, the unit could be "all commercials appearing on channels 2, 4, 5 and 7 from 8:00 to 10:00 on Sunday mornings." The categories could be frequency of commercials (e.g. sugared cereals, non-sugared cereals, toys, etc.). The schema would involve time measurements and frequency counts of the categories and indicators, recorded on a survey sheet.

Exercises for Chapter #7

Part A

1. Cite examples of status studies. Then indicate whether these studies are (or were) designed to: (a) obtain needed basic information; (b) correct misinformation; (c) collect data useful for subsequent studies; or (d) fulfill all three purposes.

2. Cite studies which will lend themselves to the casual-comparative method. What is the basic approach in setting up this type of study? How is it like and unlike a true experiment?

3. Give examples of correlational studies and list their objectives.

4. Give examples of content analysis studies and list their objectives.

5. What are the assets and liabilities of case studies?

6. Cite problems which can be fruitfully studied via the case study approach.

7. What are problems associated with the five types of descriptive studies discussed in this chapter and how can they be resolved?

Part B

Think and respond:

1. Which type of descriptive research (status, casual-comparative, correlational, case study, content analysis) is represented by each of the problems below?

2. Select one problem and suggest:

   a) appropriate operational definitions

   b) fruitful questions and/or hypotheses

   c) a research design to solve the problem – i.e. subjects to be used and techniques to be employed, type of data to be collected and their analysis.

3. What are the limitations of your research design?

Problems:

A) Which kinds of innovations are used by New Jersey school systems?

B) What causes certain people to be creative? (or to smoke excessively or to use hard drugs or to suffer heart attacks)

C) How stable are the vocational interests of adolescents?

D) Are there social class differences (or racial differences or religious differences or gender differences in the perception of the role of women?

E) What causes certain marriages to be happy?

F) What is the relationship between certain personality factors and degrees of obesity?

G) What are the dietary habits of different United States ethnic groups?

H) Are college grades good predictors of success in life?

I) Why is productivity so low in the Quitearly Factory?

J) You are a Martian asked to report to the Galaxy Council on the status of the American culture as reflected in its media. Specifically, what values do Americans adhere to? What problems are they faced with? Which level of civilization have they reached?

#8: Types of Research: Experimental

The experiment is probably the most rigorous type of research in that it represents a systematic procedure for answering the question: "What will occur under certain carefully controlled conditions?"   Although descriptive research (status, casual-comparative, correlational and case study) may determine relationships among variables, only experimental research can ascertain cause-and effect relationships. This is so because the essence of experimental research (unlike historical and descriptive research) is rigorous control of the conditions of the study. The durability of a product – for example, a television set – could be ascertained via a survey. However, the reliability of responses by consumers may be questionable. It would be better to design an experiment which will test the product (or products) under varying controlled conditions of use and abuse. Reports issued by the Consumers Union are good examples of such efforts. The "subjects" of an experiment may be human beings, animals, or material things.

The experimenter manipulates certain variables and observes how the subjects are affected by them. The experimenter must control certain other extraneous or confounding variables so that one can be sure that the effects observed can be attributed to the variable which was manipulated. For instance, in a study of the effects of different kinds of painkillers on pain reduction, the experimenter must control the extraneous variable "receiving attention" by giving placebos to one group of subjects. This must be done since many studies have shown that some people feel better when receiving any medication, even though the medication is a chemically inert substance; they are responding to "receiving attention."

Kinds of Variables

The experimenter deals with independent and dependent variables. The experimenter manipulates the independent variable (also referred to as treatment variable or stimulus) and studies its effect on the dependent variable (also denoted as criterion variable or response).

If the experiment involves human beings or animals, then we encounter another type of variable – the intervening variable. Intervening variables are those which reside within the organism (e.g. anxiety, fatigue, motivation). These modifying variables intervene between the stimulus and the response.

In the above cited example, the medication and the placebo given to different subjects is the independent variable and pain perception (i.e. subjective reports) is the dependent variable. Subjects' differential motivation to participate in the experiment would be an intervening variable.

Field vs. Laboratory Research

Consideration of the necessary degree of variable control and the desired amount of realism in the experiment are factors which help determine the experimental setting. Experimentation can take place in either a field or laboratory setting. Laboratory research provides the opportunity for complete control over variables; however, the resulting distortion of reality, the error of fractionation, may result. Field research, on the other hand, while affording a realistic and natural environment, does not permit complete control over variables.

Example: Laboratory research – In a laboratory experiment in which polishing solutions A and B are applied by machine to a piece of wood, solution B is found to provide the highest shine and best protection; however, application of this finding in the real world shows solution B to be practically unacceptable due to its finger-staining qualities.

Example: Field research – A reading experiment conducted in Happytown School is an example of field research in which children are being studied in a realistic and natural environment (classroom). However, it is usually very difficult for the researcher to manipulate the classroom structure so that many extraneous variables (another type variable which resides outside the organism) – such as dislike of teacher, sickness, and home situation, to name a few – would not affect the outcome.

The Hypothesis

After the literature has been thoroughly researched and the problem delineated, a specific testable hypothesis must be formulated. A hypothesis is a speculation about the relationship between two or more variables. Experimental research is concerned with the research hypothesis and the null hypothesis. The research hypothesis is an educated guess which states the expectations of the researcher in positive terms. The null hypothesis states that no relationship or difference exists between the variables concerned. It is a hypothesis stated in such a way that the researcher may test whether any difference observed could come about as a result of chance. It is a (no difference) statistical hypothesis set up for possible rejection. The rejection of the null hypothesis means that the corresponding research hypothesis is tenable.[1]

Example: Research hypothesis – Children who have had kindergarten experience will demonstrate greater academic achievement in the first grade than those who have not had this experience.

Example: Null hypothesis – There will be no significant difference in academic achievement in the first grade between those children who have had kindergarten experience and those who have not.

The term "significant" relates to the criterion which the researcher uses when testing the Null Hypothesis, i.e. in deciding whether to accept or reject it. For instance, if a researcher uses the .05 level of significance and, based on a calculated statistic, decides to reject the Null Hypothesis, the chance that he or she does so wrongly is 5%. Statistical significance varies with the size of the sample. The larger the sample, the more likely that the results may be statistically significant but may not be practically significant.

Operational Definitions

The behavioral and measurable terms used in an experiment must be given precise definitions. There are called operational definitions.

Example: Kindergarten experience – Attendance for one school year in a certified public school kindergarten.

Example: Academic achievement – As measured by Metropolitan Achievement Test.

Such operational definitions are essential to clarify the variables, concepts and terms which have a special meaning in a research study.

Criteria for a good hypothesis are:

1. Should be worthy of testing. Although one of the most difficult issues in research is deciding on the merits of a research question, generally speaking, the research effort does not warrant investigation based only on personal curiosity. Does the hypothesis relate to current theories, program planning, classroom practice? Or is there a clear issue that can be

---

[1] Refer to A Practical Guide to Statistics for Research and Measurement (Lang) for a fuller treatment.

illuminated by the hypothesis? Is the hypothesis reasonable and consistent with known facts and theories?

Example: <u>Unworthy</u> – Suppose you attempt to start your car and nothing happens. A hypothesis that the car will not start because you left the water running in the bathroom sink is nor reasonable. One stating that the battery is dead is plausible and worth testing.

2. <u>Should be testable</u> – This simply means that the hypothesis is verifiable; that is, that it permits the drawing of conclusions in such a way that empirical observations will either support or refute the hypothesis.

Example: <u>Not testable</u> – The Head Start Program promotes the all-around adjustment of the preschool child. This would be hard to test because of the difficulty of defining and measuring "all-around adjustment."

3. <u>Should be stated as briefly as possible, consistent with clarity</u>.

Example: <u>Unclear</u> – The effects of teacher training and experience on teacher effectiveness and success are far-reaching and highly questionable.

<u>Factors to be Considered in Setting Up the Experiment</u>[2]

In order for the experimental results to be useful, the following three major questions must be addressed:

1. To what degree has internal validity been established?

2. To what degree has external validity been established?

3. How has the sample been selected and assigned?

<u>Internal validity</u> concerns the degree to which observed occurrences in the sample are influenced by extraneous variables and attempts to answer the question: Did in fact the experimental treatment make a difference in this experiment? Following are typical extraneous variables:

a. <u>History</u> – Specific external events beyond the control of the researcher that may have a stimulating of disturbing effect upon the performance of the subjects.

---

[2] Based on Campbell and Stanley (1966).

Example: In an experiment evaluating the effects of a weight-reducing drug, certain societal stresses (e.g. inflation, threat of war) may cause certain subjects to gain or lose weight.

b. <u>Maturation</u> – Biological or psychological changes which may occur within the subjects during the experimental process.

Example: When assessing the effectiveness of certain types of counseling of therapy, passage of time and attendant physiological/psychological changes may result in conflict resolution or diminution.

c. <u>Testing</u> – If an experimenter uses a pre-test and a post-test which are similar and the time lapse between the two tests is relatively short, it is possible that subjects will show a gain in performance (e.g. mathematics) because they have become "test-wise." That is, taking the pre-test may enable them to work more efficiently on the post-test and thus obtain a higher score.

d. <u>Instrumentation</u> – A gain in performance may be attributed to a change in assessment. Thus, subjects may achieve higher scores in mathematics because an easier post-test was used (compared to the pre-test). Or, in a study calling for repeated observations of remedial teachers, observers may give progressively higher ratings because the teachers are expected to do better.

e. <u>Statistical Regression</u> – The tendency of extreme scores (high/low) to go toward the mean in re-testing. For instance, since luck is capricious, students who scored very low on a pre-test (e.g. 20th percentile) will probably earn higher scores on the post-test (i.e. shift toward the mean). Extremely high scorers on the pre-test will also shift toward the mean on the post-test. This statistical regression can be controlled if both experimental and control groups comprise subjects (via random assignment) with extremely high or low scores.

f. <u>Differential Selection</u> – The effect of the experimental treatment may be confounded because other than characteristics common to experimental and control groups may be deciding factors.

Example: In the weight reduction experiment, experimental and control groups may be formed from among subjects who are at least 30 pounds overweight. But if one experimental group contains a greater proportion of subjects with definable physical and/or psychological problems, then the outcome of this experiment is questionable. This confounding effect may be controlled by selecting experimental and control groups which are similar.

g. <u>Experimental Mortality (Attrition)</u> – Inability to consider in the data the common characteristics of subjects who drop out of a study.

Example: Subjects in experimental and control groups may differ on the post-test not because of the treatment effect (e.g. weight-reducing drug or group therapy) but because of the systematic drop-out of persons from one of the groups.

h. <u>Hawthorne Effect</u> – The introduction of bias in favor of the experimental group as a result of subject awareness of and involvement in the experiment. This confounding effect was alluded to earlier in connection with the example of receiving a "medication" believed to be potent. In another setting, the novelty of a new method or new machinery may result in short term gains, learning or output; but after the novelty wears off, no appreciable changes will be noted in student achievement or worker productivity.

These extraneous variables, among others, affect the experimental results. Random assignment of subjects to groups and selection of the appropriate experimental design help to control and thus minimize their influence.

<u>External validity</u> concerns the power of the experiment to generalize the findings derived from the sample to a target population. The target population is the population to which the researcher wishes to generalize the findings. The target population may be people (e.g. all the people in the state of New Jersey or in Essex County, or all 11th graders in Happytown High School) or things (e.g. all four-door sedans produced by Safety First Corporation or all Model 18 televisions produced by Visionnaire Corporation). Any influence which confounds the generalizability of the experiment by interfering or interacting with the experimental treatment will result in external <u>in</u>validation. The sample selected and the setting of the study, as well as other experimental characteristics, should correspond as closely and realistically as possible to the target population.

The researcher must select, assign, and thoroughly define the sample. The <u>quality</u> of the sample is the major consideration. The extent to which the sample is <u>representative</u> of the target population and clearly defined will determine its generalizability.

The primary purpose of experimental research is to discover principles that have universal application. Generalization can only be made if the researcher has selected subjects by means of appropriate sampling techniques. Random sampling, in which each individual in a defined population has an equal chance of being included, is preferably used to make a satisfactory inference possible.

The student should note the distinction between random selection of sample subjects from a target population which helps establish external validity and random assignment of sample subjects into experimental and control groups which helps establish internal validity.

Types of Samples

Simple Random Sampling

In simple random sampling, all individuals have an equal and independent chance of being selected. Winners of the New Jersey Lottery are selected in this fashion.

Systematic Sampling

In systematic sampling, subjects are not chosen independently. After the selection of the first person, all other selections are automatically determined. For instance, a 10% sampling of registered voters in Happytown is desired, and a list of voters is available. The first name is selected at random, and then every 10th name until a 10% sample is achieved.

Stratified Sampling

In stratified sampling, subjects are chosen so that certain subgroups in the target population will be represented in the sample, proportional to their number in that population. For instance, suppose that sex, race and socioeconomic status are deemed important variables in a study and that the demographic characteristic of the target population are known (i.e. the number of men and women of four racial groups and among three socioeconomic segments). Sub-samples can then be selected at random from the 24 population groupings (or strata). If 6% of the population is "male, white, upper class," then 6% of the sample subjects should fall into this special grouping.

Cluster Sampling

In cluster sampling, geographical units of people are selected rather than individuals. For instance, rather than surveying all the inhabitants of Happytown (population = 53,451), four of the 16 voting districts may be selected (randomly). This technique saves time and money. It is also appropriately used when a roster of the individuals in the population is not available.

Size and Quality of Samples

Researchers are concerned about the size and quality of their sample. A sample should be representative of the population from which it is drawn. Larger samples are needed when:

1) uncontrolled variables are present,

2) comparison among subgroups will be made (see Stratified Sampling),

3) high attrition of subjects is expected, and

4) the population is very heterogeneous on the variables being investigated.

Techniques for estimating the size of samples needed are available.[3] These techniques take into account the experimenter's willingness to tolerate certain errors in accepting or rejecting the hypothesis. Sample size alone, however, will not guarantee accuracy. Representativeness is the primary consideration in selecting a sample. A sample may be large and still be biased. For instance, a survey involving millions of people residing in a metropolitan area will be biased because these people do not represent the country as a whole. Thus, sample size will not compensate for the bias introduced through faulty sampling techniques. Representativeness should be the primary goal in sample selection.

When random sampling techniques cannot be implemented, we may have sampling bias and the validity of our results is questionable. One of the most common sampling mistakes is to use volunteers as research subjects. Merely the fact that they volunteer makes them different from persons in the population who do not volunteer. Another common mistake is to use a sample because of its convenience rater than its appropriateness.

---

[3] Refer to Winer (1991), Cohen (1988) and Kraemer and Thiemann (1987).

In selecting random samples, some degree of difference may be expected to occur between subgroups, even though statistically acceptable methods of selection are used. This sampling difference, extraneous variables, and other considerations determine the selection of the experimental design.

Experimental Design

Experimental design is the blueprint of the operations that enables the researcher to test a hypothesis by reaching valid conclusions about relationships between independent and dependent variables. That is, the experimenter attempts to control or account for the extraneous and intervening variables while manipulating the independent variable to observe its effect on the dependent variable.

Example: If an experiment were to examine the effect of the i.t.a. method of reading upon reading achievement of first grade students, the independent variable would be the i.t.a. method, the dependent variable would be reading achievement, and an intervening variable might be motivation.

The selection of the experimental design is based on the purposes of the experiment, conditions under which it may be conducted, and the type of variables to be manipulated. Experimental designs can be divided into six major groups: single group designs, control group designs with random assignment, quasi-experimental designs, factorial designs, counterbalanced designs, and ex post facto designs.

Single Group Designs

Single group designs are relatively simple to carry out; however, due to the absence of a control group, they often do not yield meaningful measures of change. Even so, this design can be used when one cannot obtain a control group and when the post-test is administered soon after the pre-test. For example, a teacher may use this approach when evaluating a certain method of teaching one unit to the class.

Usually, the t-test for correlated means is used to analyze the results of this kind of design.

Control Group Designs with Random Assignment (Parallel Designs)

Control group designs with random assignment, or parallel designs, are the most commonly used designs because the presence of a control group enables the researcher to differentiate between the influence of the treatment and the influence of extraneous variables on the dependent variable. Of many variations of control group designs, one of the most effective is the Solomon 4-group design since it permits various statistical analyses to be performed. This design also studies and defines the effect of the pre-test on the experimental treatment. An analysis of variance of the post-test scores yields the required data.

The typical pre-test/post-test control group design may be illustrated by an experiment to assess the effectiveness of certain drugs to reduce hypertension. A group of subjects (e.g. males within a certain age range, similar in general health, status, and elevation of blood pressure) are randomly assigned to one of four groups. A pre-test is administered (reading of blood pressure). Group 1 is given Drug A, Group 2 takes Drug B, Group 3 takes Drug C, and Group 4 is given a placebo. After a certain time period, all subjects are given the post-test (another reading of the blood pressure). The analysis of variance of the pre-test scores should yield a non-significant F-ratio. If one or more of the medications was effective, the analysis of post-test scores may be expected to result in a significant F- ratio. If that is the case, t-test comparisons are then appropriate to determine which of the drugs was most and least effective.

To achieve the highest degree of <u>internal validity</u>, this experiment should be conducted in a hospital. Thus, extraneous variables like "history" and "experimental mortality" can be controlled. The <u>external validity</u> of this experiment is questionable, since random selection from the target population may not be possible and feasible. Because it is unlikely that any group of males afflicted with hypertension can be coerced into participating in such an experiment, sample subjects are probably volunteers and thus not necessarily representative of hypertensive males at large.

Quasi-Experimental Designs

Quasi-experimental designs are used when random assignment is not possible. The researcher must use other alternatives to lessen the initial differences between treatment groups. This may be accomplished through the use of matching, random assignment of groups rather than individuals, or utilization of the analysis of co-variance technique.

For instance, in many experiments conducted in an educational or industrial setting, it is impossible to randomly assign students or workers into experimental and control groups. The experimenter must deal with already existing classes or worker groupings which will remain intact.

Factorial Designs

Factorial designs enable the experimenter to deal systematically with more than one independent variable; that is, more than one independent variable can be manipulated. It is possible to determine the effect of each independent variable by itself as well as the simultaneous (interaction) effect of several variables.

For example, an experimenter may wish to ascertain the effectiveness of a remedial mathematics program introduced at the 4th, 6th, and 10th grade levels. Here then we have two independent variables – the program and grade level. By using a factorial design, the experimenter can determine whether the program is effective at all grade levels or only at the 4th, 6th, or 10th grade.

Sophisticated factorial designs permit researchers to deal also with three independent variables – e.g. gender (male/female), anxiety level (high/low), and type of counseling (individual/group). One of the questions which such a design can answer is: "Is individual counseling more effective for highly anxious males than for highly anxious females?" Analysis of variance is used to analyze the data of factorial design experiments.

Counterbalanced Designs

Counterbalanced designs ("musical chairs" – rotational) attempt to achieve experimental control by exposing all subjects (in turn) to all treatments. In effect, this design represents a series of replications of the experiment. To illustrate, the hypertension experiment discussed previously involved three different drugs and four groups – three experimental and one control. In the counterbalanced design, each of the four groups would, in turn, be given Drug A, B, C and the placebo as shown on the following page.

Replication	Placebo	Drug A	Drug B	Drug C
1	Group 1	Group 2	Group 3	Group 4
2	4	1	2	3
3	3	4	1	2
4	2	3	4	1

Care must be taken that the effect of one treatment (e.g. a certain drug) does not contaminate the effect of the subsequent treatment. Data are usually processed via modified analysis of variance.

Ex Post Facto Designs

Ex post facto designs (sometimes referred to as causal-comparative designs) can be used when experimental manipulation is not possible since the effects of a naturally occurring treatment are already present. Appropriate examples are studies of possible causes of severe car accidents and ways of coping with stressful situations (e.g. loss of a loved one of a job). Obviously we cannot arrange for these calamities to happen, but we can design a study which attempts to infer (though not to prove) certain causal factors. Questions such as these may be answered, even if only in a tentative manner: "Which factors – human and mechanical – account for severe car accidents?" or "Why do certain people cope better with a stressful situation than do others?"[4]

To summarize, the basic ingredients of experimental research are: (1) testable hypotheses; (2) careful selection of experimental and control groups; (3) the manipulation of the independent variable of variables; (4) control of extraneous variables; (5) measurement of the dependent variable; and (6) selection of relevant statistical analyses.

---

[4] Causal-comparative research is discussed in more detail in Chapter #7.

Exercises for Chapter #8

1) Select <u>one</u> topic or area of interest listed below and:

a) state purpose of proposed experiment

b) list operational definitions

c) list questions and/or hypotheses relevant to proposed experiment

d) indicate methods to be used to answer questions and/or to test hypotheses (refer to Section 7, <u>Methods of the Format of the Proposal of a Research Project</u> – see Appendix B).

2) What are the limitations of your experimental research design?

<u>Suggested topics/areas of interest</u>

A) Physical exercise (e.g. jogging, cycling) and health

B) Physiological and/or psychological consequences of isolation

C) The effectiveness of mind control (in controlling anxiety or decreasing depression or increasing creativity or decreasing blood pressure)

D) Durability of product (fabric, furniture, appliance, etc.)

E) Differential effectiveness of techniques of persuasion (e.g. relating to advertising, political campaigns, change of client behavior, consumer preferences, etc.)

F) Optimum living patterns (e.g. sleep cycles, working hours, recreational pursuits, modes of transportation, modes of housing, forms of marriage, etc.)

G) Control of anti-social behavior (crime, drug addiction, prostitution, environmental pollution, etc.)

H) Effectiveness of an <u>innovative</u> technique (in teaching, administration, guidance, production, etc.)

I) Effectiveness of ... (a drug, deodorant, toothpaste, form of food packaging, etc.)

J) Differential effect of color (or noise) on productivity (or physical/psychological well-being or reducing accidents, etc.)

K) Impact of television programs on ... (reading, cognitive development, aggressive behavior, etc.)

L) If you find the choice difficult, select your own topic.

Remember, you are asked to evolve an EXPERIMENT.

#9: Methods and Tools of Research: Observation, Rating Scale, and Interview

A variety of methods and tools are at the disposal of the researcher. Depending on the problem selected, a researcher may use one tool or a combination of tools. In Chapters #9 – 11 we will discuss each method or tool with respect to:

1. the kind of research problem for which it is particularly relevant
2. its distinct assets
3. its distinct liabilities.

Observation

Observation is man's most basic tool and is used when we wish to study subjects – human or animal – in a real life setting. People often bias information they give about themselves and sometimes cannot remember accurately how an event occurred, so a researcher can use the observational method to overcome these obstacles. There are three kinds of observations: non-participant, participant, and unobtrusive.

Some examples of <u>non-participant observation</u> are viewing classroom teaching while sitting somewhere in a corner, examining crowd behavior at a soccer game, or observing children playing through a one-way vision screen. The researcher does not deliberately interact with the observed in any way.

A researcher becomes a <u>participant observer</u> when he/she interacts with the group being observed or talks to the subjects. A good example of this would be someone who wanted to do a study of sensitivity training. The researcher will get a better insight of what a T-Group is and how it functions by becoming a participant rather than interviewing people who have attended such groups or reading books or journal articles about it. The researcher remains anonymous in the group to study it and to experience it first-hand. Studies of social units such as prisons and mental institutions also lead to more valid data if participant observation is used.

Participant observation is also the basic technique of ethnographic methodology. This methodology, also referred to as qualitative or phenomenological research, is the mainstay of the anthropologist. Dissatisfied with the restrictiveness of much of the traditional research techniques, some researchers appear to be turning to what they consider to be more innovative techniques found in ethnography. This approach allows the researcher to record the subjects in their own terms. While the responses on a qualitative device such as a scaled questionnaire may be criticized as biased or faked, it is often much more difficult to dismiss, for example, an employee's opinion of an accountability system he is serving under when his feelings and observations are expressed in his own words.

One important way to gather data via this technique is by taking field notes on a protocol format. See Appendix M for an example of this form. Patton (1990) is an excellent source of detailed techniques for collecting, analyzing, and presenting data gathered in this way. Some of the basic steps are:

1. Check to see that the data are complete; if not fill in the gaps and make at least four copies. One copy is put away for safe keeping, one remains in complete form to refer to during analysis, one is to write on, and one or more are for cutting and pasting.

2. Read through the field notes to code, classify, and label the content. Some kind of classification system is crucial as a first step in content analysis, which then facilitates the search for patterns, themes, and additional hypotheses. This step is directed by the research or evaluation questions that are to be answered by the study. How did the subjects interact? What role was played by the administration? How do the subjects define their settings and explain their actions?

3. Review the literature again to compare its findings with your emerging findings, to identify other concepts and models, and to clarify theoretical perspectives.

4. Reexamine the organized data again to determine its truthfulness and the degree it may have been influenced by the lack of researcher objectivity or bias in the subjects. To what degree have the hypotheses been supported or the questions answered?

5. Write the report based on the overall purpose of the project and the specific questions of hypotheses raised. The narrative produced should be written concisely in the active voice with specific examples, yet produce a holistic picture of what was found. See the above source for model reports, additional analytic strategies, and a more detailed treatment of each step in the total process.

Finally, ethnography in its broadest sense may be defined as the science of cultural description and is best accomplished by immersing oneself in the sociocultural situation under study. Used in this sense, participant observation would involve more than just recording and analyzing participant interaction; it would also include observer-participant interaction and recognizing the impact of the contextual variables surrounding the participants. In short, well-executed ethnographic research uses a technique of disciplined subjectivity. For an excellent detailed review of the literature on this topic, see Le Compte and Preissle (1993).

The critical-incident-technique developed by Flanagan (1954) is an observational method often used to identify the specific skills associated with a specific job or role. For instance, if one wishes to specify the role of a department chairperson, a researcher may interview chairpersons and their supervisors to identify the specific behavioral "critical incidents" which reflect or characterize this position. What does a chairperson do or is expected to do? The careful collection of many "critical incidents" or samples of behavior will enable the researcher to answer this question. Based on this effort, a comprehensive fob description may emerge. Or a study can be undertaken to determine which aspects of the role of department chair are effectively carried out. The critical-incident-technique may also be applied to study a variety of behavioral patterns, such as characteristics of effective corporate or communal leaders, the identification of professional or unprofessional conduct of attorneys, or the actions of sensitive and supportive partners in a meaningful relationship.

Unobtrusive observations focus on things and events which may tell us indirectly something about the people involved. This technique is based on a study of surroundings or materials used or abused. It is a study of inanimate objects to learn about human actions. The person using the materials need not be there. Some examples are writing on the blackboard, teacher-made materials (such as assignments, tests, teaching devices), the students' written work, arrangement of classroom furniture and type of bulletin board displays. Another application of this technique would be to study the morale of teachers in a certain school by examining the absentee records for Mondays and Fridays. Vandalism of library books could also be studied in this manner by an examination of the books for signs of abuse and by studying the records of lost and non-returned books.

The major assets of observation – seeing a subject in a real life setting – has to be balanced with a number of liabilities. Four liabilities that come to mind are: (1) the researcher's perceptions may be distorted due to response set and the observer may thus lose objectivity; (2) observer interaction – that is, the degree to which the presence of the observer changes the situation being observed; (3) spontaneous events – that is, actions, words, expressions occur unpredictably so that a researcher must be willing to spend a good deal of time on observations; and (4) observer contamination – that is, the degree to which prior knowledge of the subjects may alter the observer's evaluations. A number of steps can be taken to overcome these liabilities by following these guidelines:

1. The objectives of observation should be clearly defined. This is crucial. Thus, one cannot just say, "Observe the teachers in School X and see how effective they are." Teachers play many roles, some latent and others manifest. Which of these roles can we observe? Which of these roles should be included in assessing "teacher effectiveness?" We must specify beforehand what it is that we wish to observe.

2. Observers should be trained. This can be done in simulated training exercises. The purpose of this training is to provide the same frame of reference to each observer so that each will yield comparable data. When the observers seriously disagree, then additional practice sessions are needed.

3. Observations should be recorded on an Observational Guide or Observation Schedule (see page 105). This guide is to be constructed prior to the observations. Depending on the kind of problem you may wish to study, you may be able to use and Observation Guide already developed by another researcher, such as Medley and Mitzel (1963).

4. Inter- as well as intra-reliability of observations should be ascertained. Inter-reliability is determined by comparing the observations of two or more different observers. Intra-reliability is derived from repeated observations made by the same observer.

5. In order to capture some kind of typical behavior, some scheme of time sampling should be used (see page 106). For example, a person should be observed at different time periods during the week or month over which observations extend. Why do you think that this is a good idea? The length of time period and the pattern of recording observations vary, depending on the phenomenon observed. For instance, classroom teaching may be

observed for a 50-minute period, but entries on the Observation Guide may be made at intervals of ten minutes.

6. Where possible in the case of non-participant observation, a one-way vision screen and a video recorder should be used.

7. If the observer must enter the room, he/she should not record observations during the first five to ten minutes to help control for subject reaction. It is also advisable to prepare the subjects beforehand for the visit and acquaint them generally with the study or very candidly say that the mature of the study cannot be revealed because it may affect their behavior.

In concluding this section, it is important to emphasize that there are different levels of observation. Simply recording the behavior of subjects or recording the number and location of various physical objects is less complex than evaluating and judging what is being observed. Therefore, it is important to consider beforehand what level of observation is required to solve the research problem and design the observation document accordingly.[1]

Rating Scales

A rating scale is a tool for systematic appraisal, either by the respondent or an observer. Rating scales are devices which enable us to record and to quantify our judgments of people as well as of all kinds of products. This tool may be used to assess job performance, various aspects of personality, potential for doing graduate work, or the quality of a meal. On a strictly educational level, a rating scale may be used to help motivate students, to determine how a student stands in relation to other students socially, to provide clues for academic or psychological counseling, or to provide more complete school records for counseling and parent conferences.

These scales can be used by themselves or as part of some other tool such as the observation guide, the interview, the questionnaire, a personality inventory, or a case study.

Three commonly used types of rating scales are the numerical, the graphic, and the semantic differential scale (see page 107).

---

[1] Refer to Kerlinger (1986), for additional information on observation.

The <u>numerical scale</u> is a scale dealing with quantifying judgments. Two descriptive phrases define the extreme positions of the scale; for example, "6" is very adequate and "1" is very inadequate. The rater is asked to place a check somewhere along the continuum. Based on this type of a scale, it is possible to compute means, medians, and standard deviations.

The <u>graphic scale</u> is similar to the numerical scale in that the rater places a check along some point of the continuum. However, instead of referring to numbers, short descriptive phrases are placed at different places below the line and the rater is required to read these and check the appropriate one. This kind of scale is used more in a descriptive rather than a statistical sense; that is, behavior is judged via verbal descriptions rather than by a numerical index. For instance, 100 candidates for managerial positions have undergone a training program and are rated by their trainer. The results are as follows: 10 are "natural business leaders," 35 "show good promise," 30 are "average," and 25 are "weak in leadership." The quality of the graphic scale depends on one's ability to construct meaningful phrases which can be placed along a continuum from one extreme to another.

The <u>semantic differential scale</u> consists of a set of bipolar adjectives. Persons are asked to check a space along the continuum which corresponds to their judgment. [2]

This type of scale has many applications. A person may rate himself or herself or others using a set of bipolar adjectives. A person may rate a construct like "school," "the white race," or "marriage." The applications of this scale are only limited by the imagination of the researcher. If several persons rate the same concept, profiles may be constructed showing the degrees of overlap or divergence of the ratings of each pair of adjectives.

Through the use of these scales, the researcher obtains two kinds of data: the qualitative rating assigned each item and a basis for ordering the entire set of items. The qualitative rating obtained is more thorough and specific for the verbal or graphic than the numerical scale. However, the numerical scale provides a more precise basis for ordering than does the verbal scale. Thus, a basis for deciding which scale to use is whether the primary research need is the rating of each item or the ordering of the entire set of items.

In addition, each type of rating scale involves a basic assumption. In developing the <u>graphic scale</u>, it is assumed that the researcher can find meaningful verbal labels which will

---

[2] Refer to Snider and Osgood (1969).

make clear his or her perceptions of each scale point to the extent that all respondents will see it in the same way. In the example given, the researcher assumes that the respondents interpret the words "weak in leadership" in the same way. The <u>numerical scale</u> also has an implicit assumption: that each respondent defines the number scale points as meaning the same degree of importance, so that it is reasonable to assume that three respondents who each circle "4" are referring to the same degree of importance. These assumptions can be verified by doing pilot studies and using other techniques described in the references. Including an explanation of the descriptive phrases or numerical interpretations reduces the vagueness of terms and aids in providing more reliable data.

Just as subjects are prone to be affected by response sets, so are observers and raters. The validity of the rating scale may be weakened by a number of rater response sets such as the halo effect, the generosity error, and the error of central tendency.

The <u>halo effect</u> is a tendency to let initial impressions of a person affect one's ratings of the person on other characteristics. These impressions can be favorable or unfavorable, and they can cloud the rater's mind and blind him or her to a person's true abilities in different areas. For example, a person may impress a rater with his or her honesty in matters of money, and the rater may then assume that he or she will be honest in all other areas such as taking tests in school and playing Solitaire.

A rater who consistently hands out high ratings commits the <u>generosity error</u>. This person is very lenient and his or her ratings must be examined carefully.

Another response set that can affect rating scales is the <u>error of central tendency</u>. Raters who do not wish to commit themselves one way or another or who feel that they do not have enough basis for a judgment may select categories in the middle of the scale. Their ratings usually yield a very small degree of significance in the overall study and should not be taken too seriously.

These observer or rater response sets as well as other potential misuses of the rating scale may be minimized by the following suggestions:

1. Raters should be trained in the use of the scale, particularly if it is a sophisticated one, and be cautioned against succumbing t the errors enumerated.

2. Raters must have a frame of reference such as a norm group against which they are rating people. For example, if they are to rate neophyte drafting supervisors, they are to use the performance of other neophyte drafting supervisors as their basis for comparison.

3. Traits which are to be rated must be defined operationally – that is, given a common meaning for the rater to study and watch for as he or she rates the subject. Raters should be given specific illustrations for the descriptions of each trait to be rated.

4. All persons should be rated on one trait before proceeding to the next trait. In this fashion, the rater can maintain a uniform frame of reference.

Interview

An interview is the collection of data through direct verbal interaction between individuals. It is the appropriate research tool when: (1) direct face-to-face contact with persons is imperative; (2) immediate responses are desirable; and (3) its use is feasible – one deals with a relatively small sample, adequate financial support, and availability of trained interviewers.

On the other hand, questionnaires would be used when larger samples of a population are the focus of an inquiry, when direct face-to-face contact is not deemed essential, and when funds are relatively limited.

Different types of interviews are conducted depending on the nature of the study. Interviews can be used for placement in school, college, job, branch of military service, or various organizations such as political or religious groups. Interviews are sometimes used to find out how the public reacts to a certain international or national event, or to ascertain consumer opinions in regard to various products on the market. Each of these interview situations would be conducted with a particular goal in mind, and the questions would be geared accordingly. Later in this chapter we will discuss some dos and don'ts for interviewing.

The interview can be highly structured wit a set of formal questions or it can be non-directive where questioning is less formal and depends a great deal on the responses of the person being interviewed. There are four different types of interviews. They are as follows:

1. Individual interview (one interviewer and one respondent)

2. Team interview (two or more interviewers and one respondent)

3. Group interview (group of persons being interviewed by one or more interviewers)

4. Stress interview (respondent is placed in a stressful situation either physically and/or verbally, and his or her responses are observed "under fire").

The advantages of an interview over other research tools such as a questionnaire are the flexibility to deviate from the set pattern of questions if the need arises and the ability to probe areas of interest or vagueness instead of relying on routine responses. In addition, the interview provides greater communication between the interviewer and the respondent and permits immediate checking on information.

Some of the drawbacks of this technique include the cost of the interview in terms of time and money; the problem of determining the worthwhileness of the information obtained and the truthfulness of that information; the need to create rapport between the interviewer and the respondent; and the problem of the interviewer's bias and subjectivity.

In order to prevent potential interviewers from falling into any of the above-mentioned pitfalls, the following suggestions are offered:

1. The objectives of the interview must be clearly defined beforehand and all terms operationally defined and explained to the interviewer as well as pre-tested.

2. Interviewers should be trained via simulation. This training must also stress the ethics of interviewing, such as making the client feel comfortable through small talk and assuring him or her of total confidentiality, the art of asking questions, and means of establishing good rapport.

The interviewer should not use leading questions or try to make the respondent feel ill at ease. If this happens, he or she should try using a different approach to obtain the desired information. The interviewer should also try to be aware of the subtle social pressures the respondent might be experiencing in his or her everyday life and in the interviewer's office.

Leading questions, lack of rapport, or a respondent's feeling that he or she must give socially acceptable or "right" answers will adversely affect (confound) the worthwhileness of the data obtained.

3. Responses should be recorded on an Interview Guide (see page 108) which is constructed, tested, and revised prior to the interview. The interviewer should be thoroughly familiar with and comfortable using this guide.

4. Tape recorder and /or videotape can be used during the interview with the knowledge and consent of the respondent. This eliminates the need to write during the interview and thus possibly distract the respondent. It also allows the interviewer more time to think on the spot and then get a clearer view of the interview itself as he or she later goes over the recording.

5. Evidence regarding the reliability of the interview content should be ascertained. This can be done by rewording the questions and asking them a second time. This is another means of ensuring the truthfulness and worthwhileness of the information obtained.

6. The optimum time for the interview must be ascertained. The interviewer should not make the interview too long so that the respondent becomes tired, bored or irritable. This attitude will diminish the reliability of the interview. If more information is desired, the interviewer should schedule another session with the respondent and continue where the previous interview ended.

Two concluding ideas regarding interviews are:

Silence is often far more expressive than speech. "Silent language" on the part of the interviewer as well as the respondent can be one of the most effective forms of communication. It can say things and convey feelings that could be put into words only with the greatest of difficulty – if at all. For example, a significant pause before replying, or not answering at all, can have a far more telling effect on the other person than anything one could possibly say. Silence is a powerful and often unanswerable figure of speech. Moreover, silence is one of the hardest arguments to refute.

Finally, when you are interviewing people, watch their "body language" – how they walk into the room, how and where they sit, and where they place their hands during the interview. These are some subtle clues that indicate an emotional state of which the respondent is usually totally unaware.[3]

---

[3] Suggested additional readings: Forcese and Richter (1973), and Stewart and Cash (1996).

Example: Observation Guide

What was observed?	Time Period						
	1	**2**	**3**	**4**	**5**	**6**	**7**
Clarifies feelings							
Praises or encourages							
Uses student ideas							
Asks questions							
Lectures							
Gives direction							
Criticizes constructively							
Student talk in response to teacher							
Student talk initiated by student							
Silence							
Criticizes negatively							

Example: Time Sampling

Time Period	Monday	Tuesday	Wednesday	Thursday	Friday
1			X		
2				O	
3	X				
4		O			
5					X
6		X			
7					O
8				X	
9	O				
10			O		

X = 1st week

O = 2nd week

Example: Numerical Rating Scale

To what extent do you consider the present textbooks used in your school to teach appreciation of science fiction to be adequate?

(Please place a check along the scale below.)

```
| | | | | | | | | | | | |
```

Very   Very
inadequate   adequate

Briefly explain your rating:

Example: Graphic Rating Scale

Human Relations

How effective is she in working with others?

```
|               |               |               |
```

Weak in   Average   Shows good   A natural
leadership   promise   leader

Drive

Highly motivated? Self-starter?

```
|                   |                   |                   |
```

Powerful, superior   Reasonable assur-   Slightly un-   Timid and
purpose and force   ance; has goal   sure of self   hesitant

Example: Semantic Differential Scale

Good......................Bad

Slow......................Fast

Weak..................Strong

Smart..................Stupid

Kind.....................Cruel

Afraid..................Daring

<u>Example</u>: <u>Interview Guide</u>

Hello, I am _____ from Happytown University. Many people have interesting hobbies such as collecting stamps, coins, and antiques. As people will have more leisure time, they may wish to start a hobby like collecting different things. We are trying to gather information which may help people to start collecting and thus, possibly, get more satisfaction out of life. Your answers to these few questions will be very helpful. We will regard your answers as confidential.

1. Are you collecting things?   _____ Yes   _____ No

> (If "No," thank respondent and end interview. If "Yes," continue below and hand CARD to respondent.)

2. Which of these things do you collect?

		How old when started?	Approximate hours/week
a.	_____ Stamps	_____	_____
b.	_____ Antiques	_____	_____
c.	_____ Coins	_____	_____
d.	_____ Autographs	_____	_____
e.	_____ Art works	_____	_____
f.	_____ Sport cards	_____	_____
g.	_____ Match boxes	_____	_____
h.	_____ Dolls	_____	_____
i.	_____ Miniatures	_____	_____
j.	_____ Books	_____	_____
k.	_____ Figurines	_____	_____
l.	_____ Other (indicate)	_____	_____
m.	_____ Other (indicate)	_____	_____
n.	_____ Other (indicate)	_____	_____

3. How old were you when you started collecting these items? (List above.)

4. About how many hours per week do you devote to collecting these items?
    (List above; try to get an estimate.)

5. Why did you start collecting?
    (List reasons for each item. If needed, ask: Did anyone get you started? Who?)

6. What do you find satisfying about collecting?
    (If needed, probe for personal satisfactions and investment possibilities.)

(continued on next page)

7. What, if anything, do you find dissatisfying about collecting? (If needed, probe for each item collected).

8. Do you belong to a club or organization related to your collection?

    ____ Yes   ____ No   (if "Yes," which one/s? _____)

9. Do you subscribe to a newsletter or magazine related to your collection?

    ____ Yes   ____ No   (if "Yes," which one/s? _____)

10. What advice can you give someone who wants to start collecting things? (If needed, probe for specifications on each item.)

11. During which month and year were you born? ____ (month) ____ (year)

12. How many years of education have you completed? ___ years

13. Are you generally a contented person? ____ Yes ____ No

                                    ____ Hard to say
            (Thank respondent.)

14. Gender of respondent: ____ Male ____ Female

Interviewer's name _____ Date of interview _____

1) Which studies could yield meaningful data via "participant observation?"

2) Give examples of studies which could use "unobtrusive" observations.

3) Complete a set of guidelines for controlling response sets. Apply these guidelines to evaluate instruments handed out in class. How could you minimize each of these sets?

   a) halo effect

   b) generosity error

   c) error of central tendency

4) Which type of research study calls for which type of interview?

   a) individual

   b) team

   c) group

   d) stress

5) How could the validity of the interview be improved?

#10: Methods and Tools of Research: Questionnaire

The questionnaire is a tool for soliciting and recording written responses from individuals. The questionnaire and the interview are closely related; the latter may be considered as an oral questionnaire.

The questionnaire is a useful research tool when: (1) a large sample or samples, perhaps even a population, need to be surveyed; (2) face-to-face contact is not deemed essential; and (3) limited funds are available.

Here are suggestions for constructing and using a questionnaire[1]:

1. Seek via a questionnaire only that information which cannot be obtained by other means. You will only annoy a busy respondent if he or she can justifiably say, "Why didn't that person look for this information in such and such a place?" For instance, one need not write to deans of various colleges to ascertain which curricula are offered. A careful examination of college catalogs will reveal the desired information.

2. Develop a "blueprint" for your questionnaire. This was discussed previously in connection with content validity[2]. Set down the objectives of your survey and spell out the specific information which you are seeking. Then, based on these objectives, write items which you hope will give you the information.

3. Pilot test specific questionnaire items as well as the total instrument to determine clarity of questions, ease of responding, and optimum length. Show your questionnaire to people (i.e. try it out), preferably people like those who will eventually fill out your questionnaire. For example, if the target population is principals of schools, submit a draft of your questionnaire to a group of school principals, not teachers or college professors. Where possible, sit down with these people and get their first-hand reactions.

4. Directions to respondents must be clear, unambiguous, and complete. Your pilot testing can aid you in arriving at good directions.

---

[1] Two excellent sources for ideas on questionnaire construction and use are Anderson (1986) and Sudman and Brodman (1982).
[2] Refer to Chapter #5 for an explanation of content validity.

5. Define all terms used in your questionnaire which could be misunderstood. For instance, if you use the term "disadvantaged," you should define it in terms of family income – perhaps $4000 or below.

6. Make sure that your questionnaire looks attractive – i.e. items are neatly arranged and the copies are clean and readable. This shows that you feel your study is important. If questionnaires are sloppily reproduced, you cannot expect your respondent to be very motivated to reply.

7. Design your questionnaire so that it can be easily filled out and, eventually, tabulated. If you are aiming at a large return (for example, several hundred) and you are contemplating various kinds of analyses, consider data processing (see Chapter #4).

8. Group together items which relate to specific sections on your questionnaire.

9. With multiple response items, list several common responses and include one or more categories of "Other: please specify."

Example: Which of these items do you collect? (please check)

_____ Antiques

_____ Stamps

_____ Coins

_____ Dolls

_____ Autographs

_____ Art Prints

_____ Other (please specify) _____

10. Multiple responses must be "mutually exclusive" as well as "exhaustive." "Mutually exclusive" means that each category listed must be entirely separate or independent from every other category. There should be no overlapping of categories which would confuse the respondent. Which of these examples is correct?

<u>Total Family Income</u>

_____ $25,000 and above   _____ $25,000 and above

_____ $15,000 - $25,000   _____ $15,000 - $24,999

_____ $ 8,000 - $15,000   _____ $ 8,000 - $14,999

_____ Under $8,000   _____ Under $8,000

"Exhaustive" means that every possible response must be provided for in the item. The complete range of responses must be presented. Which of these items is correct?

<u>Total Family Income</u>

_____ $25,000 and above   _____ $15,000 - $24,999

_____ $15,000 - $24,999   _____ $ 8,000 - $14,999

_____ $ 8,000 - $14,999   _____ Under $8,000

_____ Under $8,000

11. Consider supplementing your structured questionnaire items with an open-ended follow-up probe. For example:

Did you find your graduate training _____ excellent _____ very good _____ good _____ fair, or _____ poor?

Briefly explain your rating.

12. Consider including in your questionnaire a number of open-ended questions which allow your respondent some freedom of expression. For example:

To what extent do you think that your graduate training has prepared you to be a guidance counselor?

13. Avoid descriptive adjectives that have no agreed-upon meaning (e.g. "frequently," "rarely," etc.); instead, state the frequency.

Poor example: How frequently do you watch TV?

Better example: Appropriately how many hours per week do you watch TV?

_____ hours per week

14. Avoid double-barreled questions (e.g. "Do you believe that gifted students should be placed in separate instructional groups and assigned to special schools?"). In other words, make two questions out of this.

15. Avoid unwarranted and sometimes insulting assumptions (e.g. "Have you stopped beating your husband?" or "How do you explain the poor quality of your program?").

16. Include a check on your questionnaire's reliability via internal consistency[3].

17. Prepare and send a good letter of transmittal. This letter must contain:
a. the purpose of the survey
b. the importance and potential value of the survey to the respondent
c. a reasonable deadline for the expected return of the questionnaire
d. an offer to send the respondent a summary of the findings.

The letter should be polite and as brief as possible. Where appropriate, the use of an institution's letterhead and signatures of "prestige" people will enhance the impact of the survey. It should be noted that a letter of transmittal is not necessary if you are administering your questionnaire in person. However, always secure permission to distribute a questionnaire in a school or agency from the proper administrator before circulating it.

18. If possible, enclose a stamped, self-addressed envelope to facilitate returns.

19. Check on the proper timing for your mailing. Vacation periods and holiday seasons are potential detriments to getting good returns. Also, if you are planning to reach school principals, avoid the opening and closing school months.

20. Provide for several follow-ups. When doing the first follow-up, include another copy of the questionnaire. For subsequent follow-ups, use briefer versions of your questionnaire comprising the most essential items. If you are really persistent, eventually you have to settle for a postcard follow-up.

21. Check on your non-respondents. If you only get a 40% or 50% return, then you will not know whether these respondents are representative of the total sample you had planned to survey. Phone inquiries directed to a sample of non-respondents, eliciting information on certain key items, may help you determine whether your non-respondents are similar to or different from your respondents. Telegrams and mailgrams can also be used to

---

[3] Refer to Chapter #5 for an explanation of internal consistency.

check on non-respondents providing you have the money to pay for this type of communication.

22. Consider sequential mailings – i.e. requests for limited information at any given time. Thus, your respondent will not be overwhelmed by one lengthy questionnaire and be more inclined to respond to a shorter one. Subsequently, you may send out additional questionnaires accompanied by a summary of the previous survey.

A number of liabilities are associated with the use of the questionnaire, such as:

1. The researcher cannot check on the effectiveness of the communication (unlike with an interview). If, despite the pretesting of items, certain questions are unclear to the respondent, these cannot be clarified. The questionnaire "stands on its own."

2. It is difficult to check on the reliability of the responses. Honesty of replies may or may not be a valid assumption.

3. We do not know <u>who</u> actually completes the questionnaire. If someone other than the intended respondent fills it out, then the information may be less than trustworthy.

4. We have no control over <u>when</u> the respondent fills out the questionnaire. Will the respondent answer when motivated to concentrate on the task or will a slipshod job be done under less than optimum conditions?

5. Questionnaires which were filled out incorrectly or incompletely require additional follow-ups or may have to be discarded.

6. Questionnaire returns may be low (e.g. 50%), requiring several follow-ups. Considering the increasing rates of postage, expenses may mount. Also, it the study must be completed by a certain date, then the analysis – based on low returns – will yield less meaningful results.

7.   The researcher must carefully weigh pros and cons regarding collecting anonymous responses. If persons are asked to write their names, they may be inhibited in some way and their answers may not be quite truthful. However, you will be able to

undertake a follow-up study. If you do not have the respondent's name, you may get more information but you still do not really know if the responses are honest. Also, you will not be able to collect follow-up data.

In the case of the questionnaire, as with any other research tool, advantages and disadvantages must be weighed to determine whether this particular tool will provide the best chance of obtaining the data needed for the research project.

1) Select <u>one</u> topic or area of interest listed below and:

   a) state purpose of projected study

   b) list questions and/or hypotheses relevant to projected study

   c) indicate subjects to be used.

<u>Suggested topics/areas of interest</u>

A) Assessing effective teachers (or supervisors, principals, guidance counselors, car mechanics, etc.).

B) Opinions regarding a current national (or local or international) issue

C) Reactions to TV programs (or movies, bestsellers, etc.)

D) Changing roles of women and men (or parents and children, etc.)

E) Changing lifestyles (dwellings, marriages, leisure habits, occupations, etc.)

F) Opinions regarding diets, nutrition and health

G) Consumer preferences

H) Evaluation of a product (garment, machine, tool, educational equipment, etc.)

I) Study of the environment (home, school, class, community, nature, etc.)

J) Analysis of interpersonal relations (parent-child interaction, counselor-client, physician-patient, wife – husband, teacher – pupil, etc.)

K) The human condition (love, hostility, empathy, sexual compatibility, anxiety, loneliness, etc.)

L) Reactions to experiences in a foreign country

M) Assessment of leadership (in any human setting)

N) Beliefs, opinions, feelings regarding ………….

O) (Add your own)

2) Use the guidelines for questionnaire construction developed in this chapter to evaluate questionnaires handed out in class.

#11: Methods and Tools of Research:
Tests, Sociometric Measures, and Experimental Measures

We shall conclude the presentation of various methods and tools of research by discussing with you the use of tests, sociometric measures, and some available experimental measures.

Tests

A great variety of tests exists. When you take your car for its annual tune-up, it is being tested. When you go yourself to your annual medical check-up, the physician and laboratory technician subject you to a number of tests. In this discussion, we shall focus on the test as it applies to people.

One may think of the test as a <u>systematic</u> procedure for eliciting responses from one or more persons. <u>Norm-referenced</u> tests (also referred to as standardized tests) identify an individual's performance in relation to that of others on the same test. For example, Helen's score of 85 on the Sense of Humor Test places her at the 65th percentile; that is, her score was higher than 65% of those people who took this test. On the other hand, <u>criterion-referenced</u> tests identify an individual's performance with respect to an established standard or criterion of performance. For example, Adell correctly identified 70% of the famous composers included in Highnote's List of Famous Composers. While scores obtained with norm-referenced (standardized) tests are usually converted into percentiles or standard scores (to permit comparisons among people), scores on criterion-referenced tests are usually reported and interpreted on the basis of the number of items answered correctly (to permit comparison on an individual's score relative to a standard of expected performance). Since many research studies involve comparisons between groups, even criterion-referenced test scores may be used for comparative purposes. Regardless of whether a researcher uses a norm- or a criterion-referenced test, it is the <u>systematic</u> rather than the haphazard procedure which makes the test a potentially excellent research tool.

Some tests may be used as criteria in pre- vs. post-experimental comparisons. Much testing is done in schools to determine student achievement. Other tests may be used to describe characteristics of people so that those certain common traits may be selected for a research study. For example, if you are interested in determining the effect of certain experimental intervention (such as counseling) on changing self-perceptions, obviously you have to ascertain the self-perceptions of your subjects. This can be accomplished by using any one of a number of self-concept tests.

Tests are essential tools in any kind of prediction study. For instance, in order to predict job success, one must have collected some kind of testing data several years earlier. The Differential Aptitude Tests and vocational interest tests (such as the Strong Interest Inventory and the Kuder Vocational Preference Record) are useful tools.[1]

Paper-and-pencil tests present stimuli with varying degrees of structure or ambiguity. These stimuli can be words, sentences, pictures, or various kinds of pictorial shapes. Tests which contain highly structured (unambiguous) stimuli are called "non-projective"; those which present relatively unstructured (ambiguous) stimuli are called "projective."

Examples of non-projective tests are achievement and aptitude test, intelligence tests, and many personality tests (like the Edwards Personality Preference Schedule and the Minnesota Multiphasic Personality Inventory).

Three commonly used projective tests are the Rorschach Inkblot Test, the Thematic Apperception Test (consisting of pictures), and the Human Figure Drawing Test. Projective tests are based on the assumption that responses to stimuli are meaningful and measurable, that personality affects perception, and, therefore, that perceptual responses describe personality. The more ambiguous the stimulus, the more the individual projects himself or herself into it (that is, invests a neutral stimulus with meaning). The unstructured Rorschach Inkblots have no intrinsic meaning, but the person is asked to describe them. From the person's responses to these inkblots comes a Rorschach record rich in material, reflecting the person's inner needs, feelings, and concerns. These responses have to be carefully scored and interpreted by a highly trained examiner.

The sentence completion test is a semi-projective device. A good deal of structure is provided (the beginning of a sentence). However, the sentences can be completed in many

---

[1] Information on most standardized tests (intelligence, aptitude, achievement, and personality may be found in sources such as Conoley and Impara (1995), Keyser and Sweetland (1994) and Sweetland and Keyser (1991).

different ways. These completions may also give us clues regarding thoughts, feelings, and concerns of the respondent. The content of the items in the sentence completion test varies, depending on the thrust of the study. That is, if a test is to be devised for a study in reading, several items would deal with reading.

Here is an example of a sentence completion test:

Directions: Complete the following sentences to express how you really feel. There are no right or wrong answers. Put down what you think of and proceed as quickly as you can.

1) Today I feel . . .
2) I get angry when . . .
3) People think I . . .
4) I don't know how . . .
5) I hope I never . . .
6) I can't understand why . . .
7) The future looks . . .
8) I look forward to . . .
9) If I had my way . . .
10) I wish someone would help me . . .

Such a test can be analyzed by quantifying the responses and placing them into logical categories such as "positive," "neutral," "negative," or "inner-directed" vs. "outer-directed."

In addition to the thousands of paper-and-pencil tests, we also have a variety of performance tests sometimes refereed to as "situational tests." People are tested while performing their job or under conditions which simulate their job.[2] One of these situational tests is the in-basket test, designed to simulate administrative tasks. This test consists of a collection of items such as memoranda, phone messages, reports, etc. which have accumulated in the in-basket of an administrator and are awaiting his or her attention. Two aspects of decision-making are assessed: (1) the ability to assign priorities to items requiring

---

[2] Consult U.S. Office of Strategic Services (1948) and Byham and Bobin (1973) for more information on situational tests. See also Gronlund and Linn (1989) for an up-to-date treatment of the construction of performance tests.

action; and (2) the ability to arrive at the correct decision when dealing with each item. Judges evaluate the decisions made by the person on the in-basket items.

We have referred before to standardized tests, most of which are listed and reviewed in the collection of Mental Measurements Yearbooks (e.g. Conoley and Impara, 1995). A standardized test reflects a sophisticated level of development and usage which imbue it with certain desirable characteristics. First, it has reached a relatively high degree of objectivity in its administration and scoring; thus, the beliefs or biases of the person using the test have less chance of distorting the results. Second, a standardized instrument is one for which normative data are available. That is, the test developer has administered the instrument to carefully selected samples, thus providing the user a way to analyze his or her group relative to another group. Finally, a standardized test has usually reached the point where considerable evidence has been gathered describing its reliability and validity. These are two very important characteristics which the researcher must consider in all instruments.

Two important assets of the test as a research tool are efficiency of getting needed data and ability to quantify responses. Some of the drawbacks are the time, money, and expertise needed to develop valid and reliable tests and the specialized training needed to administer and interpret certain tests, particularly projective tests. As a neophyte researcher, you need guidance in selecting the appropriate test for your study from the gamut of tests already available. In rare instances, you may need to construct your own test.

<u>Sociometric Measures</u>

Sociometric measures are methods used to collect and analyze data on the choice, communication, and interaction patterns of individuals in groups. Peer nominations and ratings are solicited by a researcher (or teacher, shop foreman, sensitivity trainer or anyone else interested in group interaction) for a variety of purposes such as:

- to set up work groups
- to arrange play groups
- to study changes in the group structure
- to identify chains of communication
- to identify persons with certain characteristics such as leadership, kindness, honesty, or obnoxiousness.

In the sociometric test, members of a group are asked to indicate their choices (first, second, third, etc.) of other members in response to a question like "With whom would you like to work?" The choices are usually recorded on a sociometric matrix and depicted on a sociogram (see page 124 for an example of each). The data derived from a sociometric test must be interpreted cautiously. While we will learn which group members are accepted or not accepted, we will not know the reasons for this. Popularity, or lack of it, is not always an asset. The "isolate" (one who was not chosen by anyone) may be quite well adjusted. Moreover, sociometric results may shift quickly, particularly if young children are asked for their preferences. Yet sociometric results are inherently valid, denoting <u>expressed</u> choices by group members at a <u>specified</u> time.

The Guess-Who technique is another commonly used sociometric measure to assess interpersonal perceptions. Group members are asked to nominate others whom they feel fit certain descriptions. Typical descriptive items are shown on page 124. This technique provides more specific data about group members than does the sociometric test. Very often, both techniques are used together. The Guess-Who technique may shed light on why group members select a leader, reject another member, or form cliques.

Experimental Measures

There exist thousands of research tools such as tests, questionnaires, attitude scales, checklists, and rating scales which have been developed for specific studies but are not well known. Nor have they been standardized and thus will not be found in the Mental Measurements Yearbooks. These tools were developed by researchers to be part of master's theses or doctoral dissertations, or for special projects. Prior to investing time and money into constructing your own tool, ascertain if someone else has already developed one that you can use. You may be able to modify an experimental measure to suit your specific purpose. If you plan to do that, be sure to obtain permission from the author and/or publisher to do so.

Experimental measures may be located in various sources such as:

1. Directories and handbooks:

    <u>Measures of social psychological attitudes</u> (Robinson et al. – 1973)

    <u>Tests and measurements in child development: Handbook II</u>

    (Johnson and Bommarito – 1971)

Tests and measurements in child development: Handbook II
(two volumes, Johnson – 1976)

Directory of unpublished experimental mental measures
(Goldman et al.) (1974 –1995)

Gender roles: A handbook of tests and measures (Beere, 1990)

Sex and gender issues: A handbook of tests and measures
(Beere, 1990)

Handbook of measurement for marriage and family therapy
(Fredman and Sherman, 1987)

2. Educational Testing Service, Princeton, NJ 08540.

(ETS maintain an extensive, up-to-date library of tests and other measurement
devices and will provide information upon request. ETS publishes the Test
Collection Bulletin and various test bibliographies such as Self-Concept Measures
K-6, 7-above; Assessment of Teachers; Criterion-Referenced Measures; and
Measures for Educationally Disadvantaged Adults.)

3. Convention programs of your professional organization. Newly developed devices
are often introduced at conventions.

3. Appendixes of project reports, like ESEA Chapter I projects. Research tools
specially developed for the study are usually presented in the report's appendix.

Example: <u>Sociometric Matrix</u>

		A	B	C	D	E	F
Brian	A		2	1	3		
Ken	B	1			2	3	
Judy	C	1	3			2	
Adell	D	1	2	3			
George	E	1		2	3		
Kirk	F	1		3	2		
1st choice	(3)	5	0	1	0	0	0
2nd choice	(2)	0	2	1	2	1	0
3rd choice	(1)	0	1	2	2	1	0
Total points		15	5	7	6	3	0

Example: <u>Sociogram</u>

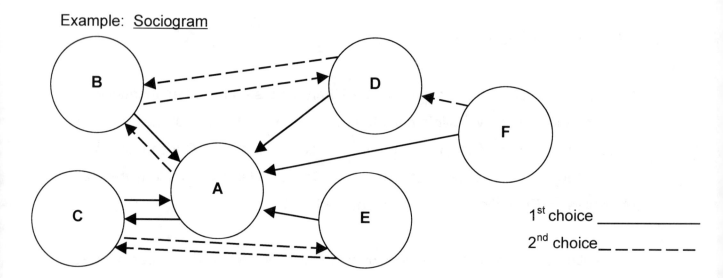

1st choice _____

2nd choice _ _ _ _ _ _ _

Example: <u>Guess-Who Technique</u>

1. This one is always picking on others and annoying them:

2. This is a person who always wants to have his/her own way:

3. This is a person who is well liked and has lots of friends:

4. Here is someone you can always count on:

5. Here is someone who is very undependable:

6. Here is someone who is very sneaky:

7. This is a person in whom I can confide:

124

1) Think of a study for which you would use the sentence completion test. Write the test items and indicate how you would score them.

2) Think of a study which may require a projective test. Construct such a test and indicate how you would analyze your results.

3) Devise some "situational" tasks which could be used to test applicants for positions as _____. How would you evaluate the completion of these tasks?

4) Which kinds of studies would lend themselves to the use of sociometric measures?

5) Construct a sociometric matrix and a sociogram.

6) Use the Guess-Who technique in this class.

7) Consult several directories and handbooks which list experimental measures.

8) Prepare an appropriate research tool (Observation Guide, Rating Scale, Interview Guide, Questionnaire, or Test) and:
   a) develop the tool
   b) propose ways and means of getting validity and reliability data
   c) suggest appropriate statistical tools for analyzing the response.

#12: The Research Report

The research report is a means by which researchers communicate to professionals the product of their efforts. It attempts to explain the problem investigated, procedures used in finding a solution, results obtained, conclusions reached, and overall generalizations and implications of the study. This report will (and should) be critically evaluated by fellow scholars. The various components of the report should be presented clearly and accurately so that the study can be replicated.

Format

The format to be used depends on the type of research[1] and the nature of the publication (journal article, monograph, thesis, dissertation, report submitted to a funding agency, report issued by an organization, etc.). We suggest that you obtain the appropriate style guide and follow published models. For instance, may colleges and universities issue guidelines for writing the thesis or dissertation. Several professional organizations such as the American Psychological Association issue their own publication manual (see APA,1994). Shown below is a typical format of a descriptive or an experimental research report:

```
Title Page
Preliminary Section
        Preface or Acknowledgements
        Table of Contents
        List of Tables
        List of Figures
Main Section
        I.      INTRODUCTION
                Problem
                Related Research
                Objectives
                Hypotheses and/or Questions Posed
                Assumptions
                Operational Definitions
        II.     METHOD
                Population
                Sample
                Research Instruments and/or Apparatus
                Procedure
        III.    RESULTS AND CONCLUSIONS
```

---

[1] See Chapter #6 for a discussion of formats used in historical, documentary, construction, and bibliographical research. Refer also to Appendixes I, J, K and L.

Content of Each Section of Research Report

Title Page

This page lists at least the title of the research study, the author's name, and the date of printing. Additional information may appear in the case of a thesis, dissertation, or report submitted to a funding agency. In the case of such specialized reports, specifications should be adhered to. The title of the report should be specific, concise, descriptive, and meaningful.

Preface or Acknowledgements

This section is optional. You may wish to record thanks to people who assisted you in the study and to convey some personal message which provides the setting for the research to be reported on.

Table of Contents, List of Tables, List of Figures, Organization of Report

These items are included as needed by the scope of the report. They are omitted in journal articles.

While the specific organization may vary for different kinds of research reports, the main components common to all reports are Introduction, Method, Results and Conclusions, Discussion, and Summary.

Introduction

Problem. Discuss the nature, scope, and significance of your study and its theoretical framework. Show how your project is related to broader problems in the area. Indicate your delimitations and state precisely the purpose of your study.

Related Research. Present a critical, comprehensive review of related research. This review should be analytical, not merely cumulative; the cited studies should be evaluated, not just listed. Report them in sufficient detail (i.e. purpose, design, findings, conclusions, strengths, limitations). Also, don't list one study after another in a boring one-study-to-a-paragraph fashion. Instead, integrate and synthesize the various studies by grouping them under appropriate headings according to topics or common themes. Show the relation of the reviewed studies to your problem, hypotheses/questions, assumptions, and procedures. Be sure that most of the studies cited are recent and that all of the are relevant! Conclude your review of related research with a succinct summary.

Objectives. Sate the specific objective(s) of your study by enumerating them.

Hypotheses and/or Questions Posed. You may either state hypotheses to be tested or questions to be answered. Occasionally, a researcher may list both. Either the research or the null hypothesis may be stated. Listing them both would be redundant.

Assumptions. The assumptions implicit in your study should be spelled out so that your reader can determine whether these are reasonable and justifiable.

Operational Definitions. Clearly define the key variables, concepts, and terms which have a special meaning in your proposed study. Do not include mere semantic definitions.

Method

This section should be especially clear and precise so that your reader knows exactly what was done. The presentation of the methodology should be detailed enough to permit a replication of the study.

Population. Indicate the nature, sources, size, and characteristics of the population from which one or more samples were drawn.

Sample. Do the same for your sample(s). Indicate your sampling method (e.g. random, stratified, cluster, volunteer, etc.).

<u>Research Instruments and/or Apparatus</u>. Describe in detail the instruments and/or equipment which were used. Report the instruments' validity and reliability. For newly developed instruments (e.g. questionnaires and attitude scales), indicate the steps taken to devise and to evaluate them. Copies of newly constructed instruments, cover and follow-up letters should be placed in the Appendix.

<u>Procedure</u>. Report fully the research design (plan of operation) and statistical techniques used. Indicate chronologically all the steps of your research effort.

Results and Conclusions

This section is reserved for the presentation of your findings and the conclusions you derive from them. These matters are <u>objective</u> and, barring a mistake in data analysis, your readers should generally arrive at the same conclusions. Interpretations of your findings are reserved for the Discussion section since these tend to be <u>subjective</u> and your readers may or may not agree with you.

Present your findings in the order in which your hypotheses and/or questions were posed. Restate each hypothesis and question, present the evidence, and state your conclusion. "Significant" as well as "non-significant" findings should be presented because your reader is entitled to get the whole story. In addition to your major findings (those pertaining to your hypotheses and/or questions), there may be minor findings. These are unexpected and incidental findings, but may be as interesting or even more interesting than your major findings. The discovery of penicillin was an unexpected, incidental finding which, of course, in subsequent years has emerged as a major research contribution. Therefore, all of your findings should be presented.

Small tables and figures should be incorporated into the body of the text. Large tables and figures should be shown on separate pages. If you plan to present a series of tables and figures, these are then best included in the Appendix in order not to clutter up your discourse. Consult APA (1994) or look over models found in your professional journals for aid in constricting tables and figures.

Discussion

Here you should address questions such as: What do the findings mean? To what extent do your findings apply beyond your situation? What deficiencies does your study have and how serious are they? Where do we go from here – i.e. which avenues of further research should be explored? This is the most creative section of the report. It is your opportunity to speculate about the meaning of your findings and to weave a meaningful picture. In the preceding sections you served as the research "technician," and here you should emerge as the research "artist."

Summary

This section is probably most widely read and is often consulted initially by readers to determine the relevance of the study to their particular needs. In a paragraph or two, briefly review your problem, methodology, results, and conclusions.

Appendix

Included here are copies of newly developed instruments, cover and follow-up letters, drawings of apparatus used, detailed tables and figures, illustrative case studies, etc. That is, the Appendix is the depository for all those materials which are too lengthy and, if included in the main body of the report, would interfere with a smooth presentation.

References – Bibliography

Include those sources actually cited in your report and perhaps others of significance. An example of a list of references is shown on pages 133 – 135.

Writing the Report

Characteristics of a Good Research Report

On page 137 we have presented a <u>Checklist for Evaluating a Research Report</u>. If the answers to the questions posed in this checklist are generally "yes," then you have produced a good report.

Some Common Errors in Interpreting Data

Beware of errors which are apparent in many research reports:

1. <u>Failing to see the significance of the data</u>. Just like some of us don't see "the woods because of the trees," so some researchers get bogged down in the minutia of their data and don't perceive the "gestalt," the essence, the totality. Also, we must distinguish between the "statistical" and "practical" significance of our data.

2. <u>Drawing incorrect inferences and conclusions</u>. One may be tempted to over-generalize. Also, if one's biases are not controlled, conclusions are arrived at which may not be based on the data presented.

3. <u>Overlooking contrary evidence</u>. You may be so intent on "proving" your hypothesis that you disregard inconvenient, contrary data. "Non-significant" data may be significant to your reader, and you should not withhold them from perusal.

4. <u>Disregarding the limitations of the study</u>. All studies have shortcomings; these should be recognized. Unexpected obstacles may alert your reader to what should be anticipated when planning similar studies.

Style of Writing

Effective writing is objective, succinct, and interesting. Many research reports employ language designed to impress the audience. As a result, such reports are stilted, snobbish, and boring. They need not be so. Use a guide like Strunk and White (1995) to develop an effective style. Do not be afraid to show your sense of humor; it will help maintain your reader's attention. Write an interesting report!

Remember, however, that objectivity is a prime concern of research. Objectivity may be diminished by using such personal pronouns as I, we, you, my, our, or us. Professionalism dictates the use of third person phrases such as "this writer" or "the researcher."

Show drafts of your report to friendly critics for commentary. By all means, proofread your report prior to its release to anyone.

Headings

Paper use of headings increases the clarity and readability of the report. Dividing the manuscript into meaningful parts compels the writer to clarify and organize his or her own thinking. Usually the report is first divided into chapters according to its primary parts. Chapters are introduced with <u>centered</u> <u>headings</u> written in full capitals. Subdivisions of chapters are made by free standing <u>side</u> <u>headings</u> (flush with the left margin) and indented <u>paragraph</u> <u>headings</u>. The three levels of headings are illustrated below:

II.   METHOD

Research Instruments

<u>Space Travel Aptitude Test</u>. Since no pertinent test was available, the researcher had to develop one … etc.

If a research report requires four levels of headings, then the following example should be followed:

II.   METHOD

Research Instruments

Space Travel Aptitude Test

<u>Validity</u>. The validity of this test was determined by … etc.

<u>Reliability</u>. Two kinds of reliability data are available … etc.

Form of Citing References

References may be cited in various ways. These are discussed in excellent sources, such as APA (1994) and Campbell et al. (1990).

Shown below are illustrative examples based on APA (1994).

Citing References: Illustrative Examples

Jones (1997), in a study of 1,462 Martian and Earthling college students, found highly significant differences between smokers and non-smokers with respect to certain personality variables. However, the results of other studies (Satan, 1996; Smith, 1995a) have been inconclusive.

Berkson (1992), Filter (1996), and Meek (1997) suggest that such genotypic factors as constitution and temperament might predispose some creatures to become smokers and also predispose them to lung cancer.

Satan (1996) considers smoking as "just another form of self-destruction" (p.13).

Smith (1995b) observed:

> Of one believes that the effectiveness of anti-smoking educational campaigns will increase as more is learned concerning the psychodynamics of smoking, then it becomes important to determine whether information now available from studies of cyborgs can be used to guide campaigns directed at adult Earthlings. (p.1313)

Following leads suggested by Smokey (1993), Bear (1997) studied consumer reactions to smoking-related TV commercials.

An excellent treatment of this is found in Lung (1993).

References

Bear, A. L. (1997, February). Are TV commercials obnoxious? Paper presented at the meeting of the Society for a Clean America, Utopia, NJ.

Berkson, J. (1992). Smoking, education and lung cancer. Glen Ridge, NJ: Glen Ridge University. (ERIC Document Reproduction Service No. ED 007 485)

Filter, O. K. (1996). Brain transplants and smoking (2nd ed.). New York: McGraw-Hull.

Jones, O. Y. E. (1997). Personality characteristics of selected groups of smokers and non-smokers (Doctoral Dissertation, Federated University of Mars). Dissertation Abstracts International, 38, 4071A-4072A. (University Microfilms No. 100-33, 812)

Lung, N. O. (Ed.) (1993). The mess media: an agonizing reappraisal. Wasteland, MO: Pessimist Press.

Satan, X. Y. Z. (1996). To roast or not to roast. Journal of Metaphysics, 13, 7-77.

Smith, B. M. (1995a). Relationship between personality and smoking behavior among Earthlings. Journal of Consoling Parapsychology, 33, 45-48.

Smith B. M. (1995b). Relationship between personality and smoking behavior among cyborgs. Stargazers Quarterly, 14, 1312-1333.

Smokey, S. (1993). Development and validation of a TV Obnoxiousness Scale. In N. O. Lung (Ed.), The mess media: an agonizing reappraisal (pp. 250-265). Wasteland, MO: Pessimist Press.

Meek, I. M. (Personal communication, April 1, 1997) – DO NOT INCLUDE IN REFERENCES BUT CITE IN BODY OF TEXT.

Other Examples

1. Citation from a secondary source

    If Dr. Lovehappy's research was located in a secondary source, refer to it as follows:
    Lovehappy (cited in Strong, 1997) fond that smoking is inversely related to sex appeal.

    Strong is listed: Strong, U. C. (1997). Romance and smoking. Tobaccoville, NC: Macmullan.

2. Government publication (corporate author; author as publisher)

    U.S. Government Printing Office (1986). Style manual (rev. ed.). Washington, DC: Author.

3. Government publication (committee as author)

    Advisory Committee to the Surgeon General of the Public Health Service (1964). Smoking and health. (Public Health Service Publication No. 1103) Washington, DC: U.S. Government Printing Office.

4. <u>Unpublished material</u>

Pype, G. D. (1997). <u>Sexual potency of smokers and non-smokers.</u>
Unpublished manuscript. (Available from ... [author's address]).

5. <u>Monograph</u>

Ceegar, G. (1996). Effectiveness of behavior modification in breaking tobacco
addiction. <u>Astrological Monographs</u>, <u>13</u>, (3, Serial No. 113).

6. <u>Magazine article (no author)</u>

Lung pollution (1998, February 29). <u>Time</u>, pp. 43-44.

7. <u>Newspaper article (no author; discontinuous pages)</u>

Tenth reunion of ex-smokers (1996, December 31). <u>Middlesex Record</u>, pp. 1, 12.

Some Final Suggestions

1. Read good models of research reports issued in your field.

2. Keep writing aids handy (e.g. dictionary, thesaurus, style manual, etc.).

3. Be prepared to write several drafts of you report.

4. Proofread all drafts of your report.

5. Solicit and expect constructive criticism of your writing.

Checklist for Evaluating a Research Report

<u>The Title</u>:

    1. Is the title concisely stated?

    2. Does the title convey the content of the study?

I.   <u>Introduction</u>

    A. <u>Statement of Problem</u>

        1. Is the problem significant?

        2. Is the problem clearly and completely formulated?

        3. Is the general scope or setting of the study adequately presented?

        4. Is the purpose of the study precisely stated?

    B. <u>Related Research</u>

        1. Is previous research related to the study presented by the investigator?

        2. How relevant is the cited research to the study presented?

        3. Is the previous research integrated or merely enumerated?

        4. Is a succinct and meaningful summary presented?

    C. <u>Hypotheses or Questions</u>

        1. Are the hypotheses to be tested or the questions to be answered clearly stated?

        2. Are the hypotheses stated in a form that permits them to be tested?

        3. Are the hypotheses or questions superficial?

    D. <u>Assumptions and Delimitations</u>

        1. Are the assumptions underlying the study made explicit?

        2. Are these assumptions reasonable?

        3. What are the implicit assumptions of the study which should have been made explicit?

        4. How has the study been narrowed down?

(continued on next page)

E. Operational Definitions

    1. Are key concepts or terms clearly defined or explained?

    2. Are the definitions or explanations meaningful?

II. Method

  A. Population and Sample

    1. Are the characteristics of the selected population and sample (size, source, nature, etc.) fully presented?

    2. Is the sampling method indicated?

  B. Research Instruments and/or Apparatus

    1. Are the techniques employed (e.g. interview, questionnaire, apparatus, tests, etc.) clearly and fully described?

    2. Are the instruments or techniques appropriate for collecting the data?

    3. If tests were used, what evidence is presented regarding their rationale, reliability, and validity?

  C. Procedure

    1. Is the design or procedure clearly and fully reported?

    2. Is the statistical treatment of data discussed?

    3. Are appropriate statistical methods used in analyzing the data?

    4. Can the study be replicated?

III. Results and Conclusions

    1. Are the findings intelligibly reported in textual presentation?

    2. Are the conclusions logically drawn (i.e. based on the data presented)?

    3. Are the tables and figures used appropriately?

IV. Discussion

    1. Are the findings discussed adequately and meaningfully?

    2. Does the investigator indicate the possible implications of the study?

    3. Are the implications meaningful?

    4. Are limitations of the study recognized?

    5. How severe are the limitations of the study?

6. What are the limitations which were not mentioned?

7. Are any suggestions offered regarding avenues for further research?

8. Are these suggestions worthwhile?

9. What other suggestions should have been offered?

V.   <u>Summary</u>

1. Are the problem and methodology restated?

2. Are the major findings, generalizations, implications and limitations succinctly synthesized?

<u>Communication</u>

1. Is the report well organized?

2. Is the report well written?

APPENDIX B
Format of the Proposal for a Research Project

Please make <u>two</u> copies of the proposal: one for you and the other for your instructor.

Hand your proposal as follows:

Your name	Draft No. _____
503 Section _____	Date submitted

The proposal should be presented in detail using the following <u>headings</u>:

1. <u>Title</u>

   State the tentative title of your proposal. Make it specific, concise, and distinctive.

2. <u>Problem – Introduction</u>

   Discuss the importance or significance of the problem selected. Show how your project is related to broader problems in the area. State the purpose(s) of the study.

3. <u>Related Research</u>

   Present a <u>critical</u> review of related research (the more technical aspects), not just a summary of the findings. Show the relation of the reviewed material to your problem, hypotheses, questions, assumptions, and procedures. Use the <u>Checklist for Evaluating a Research Report</u> as your guide. Group related research under common topical headings. For historical, documentary and construction type projects refer to page 67.

4. <u>Operational Definitions</u>

   Clearly define the key variables, concepts, and terms which have a special meaning in your proposed study. Do not include mere semantic definitions.

5. <u>Assumptions – Delimitations</u>

   Make explicit the assumptions (generalizations taken for granted) underlying various phases of your study. How has the study been narrowed down or delimited? This is usually done by time, number, location, etc.

6. Hypothesis(es) or Question(s)

Clearly state the hypothesis(es) and/or question(s) to be investigated. Make sure that your hypotheses can be tested and the questions can be answered in your study.

7. Method[1]

State clearly and fully the methods to be used in gathering data to test hypotheses and/or to answer questions posed in Section 6.

a. Subjects: Indicate nature, sources, characteristics, and size of population and sample to be used. The sample may comprise children, adults, animals, primary and secondary material (in historical research), courses of study, TV programs, etc.

Describe your sample in terms of factors such as age, gender, socioeconomic status, ethnic group, or any other variable of potential significance.

b. Techniques – Instruments: Indicate techniques to be used (e.g. experimentation, questionnaire survey, interview survey, drawings, observations, analysis of published evidence, examination of documents via internal and external criticism, etc.). Instruments not commonly used should be described in detail, giving information concerning validity and reliability. Instruments to be devised by the investigator should be pretested and examined for utility before suggesting them as methods of measurement.

c. Research Steps: List all research steps in the order in which they are to be carried out as well as time estimates for every step.

d. Data Analysis: State appropriate methods of analyzing your data (i.e. specify the statistical methods to be used for testing each hypothesis or for answering each question). Indicate the criterion of significance. Common statistical procedures like product-moment correlation, analysis of variance, t, F or Chi Square tests need not be elaborated further. However, unusual statistical procedures should be fully explained.

---

[1] For historical, documentary and construction type projects, refer to page 156.

For non-statistical type of research, indicate qualitative methods of analyzing your data.

8. Results, Conclusions, Generalizations, Implications, Limitations, Suggestions

   a. Results and Conclusions: State probable findings and conclusions.

   b. Generalization: Indicate the extent to which your results and conclusions may be found in other populations and samples.

   c. Implications: What can be learned from your study?
      What course of action seems indicated?

   d. Limitations: What deficiencies does your study have? How serious are they?

   e. Suggestions for Further Research: Indicate avenues for further research.

9. References or Bibliography
   Follow recommendations listed in Chapter #12.

———————————

Submit a dark copy.

Did you present all sections of the proposal?

Did you compare your proposal with the Evaluation Form?

Did you proofread your proposal?

APPENDIX C

ERIC Clearinghouses

ADULT, CAREER, AND VOCATIONAL EDUCATION
The Ohio State University
1900 Kenny Road
Columbus, Ohio 43210-1090
Phone: 614-292-4353
Toll Free: 800-848-4815
Fax: 614-292-1260
E-Mail: ericacve@magnus.acs.ohio-state.edu
http://coe.ohio-state.edu/cete/ericacve/index.html

ASSESSMENT AND EVALUATION
The Catholic University of America
210 O'Boyle Hall
Washington, DC 20064-4035
Phone: 202-319-5120
Toll Free: 800-GO4-ERIC
Fax: 202-319-6692
E-Mail: eric_ae@cua.edu
Gopher: gopher.cua.edu, Special Resources
http://www.cua.edu/www/eric_ae

COMMUNITY COLLEGES
University of California at Los Angeles
3051 Moore Hall
P.O. Box 951521
Los Angeles, CA 90095-1521
Phone: 310-825-3931
Toll Free: 800-832-8256
Fax: 310-206-8095
E-Mail: ericcc@ucla.edu
http://www.gseis.ucla.edu/ERIC/eric.html

COUNSELING AND STUDENT SERVICES
School of Education
University of North Carolina at Greensboro
201 Ferguson Building
Greensboro, NC 27412-5001
Phone: 910-334-4114
Toll Free: 800-414-9769
Fax: 910-334-4116
E-Mail: ericcas2@dewey.uncg.edu
http://www.uncg.edu/~ericcas2

DISABILITIES AND GIFTED EDUCATION
The Council for Exceptional Children
1920 Association Drive
Reston, VA 20191-1589
Phone: 703-264-9474
Toll Free: 800-328-0272
TTY: 703-264-9449
Fax: 703-620-2521
E-Mail: ericec@cec.sped.org
http://www.cec.sped.org/ericec.htm

EDUCATIONAL MANAGEMENT
5207 University of Oregon
1787 Agate Street
Eugene, OR 97403-5207
Phone: 541-346-1684
Toll Free: 800-438-8841
Fax: 541-346-2334
E-Mail: ppeile@oregon.uoregon.edu
http://darkwing.uoregon.edu/~ericcem

ELEMENTARY AND EARLY CHILDHOOD EDUCATION
University of Illinois at Urbana-Champaign
Children's Research Center
51 Gerty Drive
Champaign, IL 61820-7469
Phone: 217-333-1386
Toll Free: 800-583-4135
Fax: 217-333-3767
E-Mail: ericece@uiuc.edu
Gopher: ericps.ed.uiuc.edu
URL: http://ericps.crc.uiuc.edu/ericeece.html
NPIN URL: http://ericps.ed.uiuc.edu/npin/npinhome.html (National Parent Information Network)

HIGHER EDUCATION
The George Washington University
One Dupont Circle, NW, Suite 630
Washington, DC 20036-1183
Phone: 202-296-2597
Toll Free: 800-773-3742
Fax: 202-452-1844
E-Mail: eriche@eric-he.edu
URL: http://www.gwu.edu/~eriche/

INFORMATION AND TECHNOLOGY
Syracuse University
4-194 Center for Science and Technology
Syracuse, NY 13244-4100
Phone: 315-443-3640
Toll Free: 800-464-9107
Fax: 315-443-5448
E-Mail: eric@ericir.syr.edu; askeric@ericir.syr.edu
Gopher: ericir.syr.edu
AskERIC: http://ericir.syr.edu
ERIC/IT: http://ericir.syr.edu/ithome

LANGUAGES AND LINGUISTICS
Center for Applied Linguistics
1118 22nd Street, NW
Washington, DC 20037-1214
Phone: 202-429-92992
Toll Free: 800-276-9834
Fax: 202-659-5641
E-Mail: eric@cal.org
http://www.cal.org/ericcll

READING, ENGLISH, AND COMMUNICATION
Indiana University
Smith Research Center
2805 East 10th Street, Suite 150
Bloomington, IN 47408-2698
Phone: 812-855-5847
Toll Free: 800-759-4723
Fax: 812-855-4220
E-Mail: ericcs@indiana.edu
Gopher: gopher.indiana.edu
http://www.indiana.edu/~eric_rec

RURAL EDUCATION AND SMALL SCHOOLS
Appalachia Education Laboratory
1031 Quarrier Street
P.O. Box 1348
Charleston, WV 25325-1348
Phone: 304-347-0400
Toll Free: 800-624-9120
TTY: 304-347-0401
Fax: 304-347-0487
E-Mail: lanhamb@ael.org
http://www.ael.org/erichp.htm

SCIENCE, MATHEMATICS, AND ENVIRONMENTAL EDUCATION
The Ohio State University
1929 Kenny Road
Columbus, OH 43210-1080
Phone: 614-292-6717
Toll Free: 800-276-0462
Fax: 614-292-0263
E-Mail: ericse@osu.edu
Gopher: gopher.ericse.ohio-state.edu
http://www.ericse.org

SOCIAL STUDIES/SOCIAL SCIENCE EDUCATION
Indiana University
Social Studies Development Center
2805 East 10th Street, Suite 120
Bloomington, IN 47408-2698
Phone: 812-855-3838
Toll Free: 800-266-3815
Fax: 812-855-0455
E-Mail: ericso@indiana.edu
http://www.indiana.edu/~ssdc/eric-chess.html

TEACHING AND TEACHER EDUCATION
American Association of Colleges for Teacher Education
One Dupont Circle, NW, Suite 610
Washington, DC 20036-1186
Phone: 202-293-2450
Toll Free: 800-822-9229
Fax: 202-457-8095
E-Mail: ericsp@inet.ed.gov
http://www.ericsp.org/

URBAN EDUCATION
Teachers College, Columbia University
Institute for Urban and Minority Education
Main Hall, Room 303, Box 40
New York, NY 10027-6696
Phone: 212-678-3433
Toll Free: 800-601-4868
Fax: 212-678-4012
E-Mail: eric-cue@columbia.edu
http://eric-web.tc.columbia.edu

ART EDUCATION
Indiana Universities
Social Studies Development Center
2805 East 10th Street, Suite 120
Bloomington, IN 47408-2698
Phone: 812-855-3838
Toll Free: 800-266-3815
Fax: 812-855-0455
E-Mail: ericso@indiana.edu
http://www.indiana.edu/~ssdc/art.html

CHILD CARE
National Child Care Information Center
301 Maple Avenue West, Suite 602
Vienna, VA 22180
Phone: 800-616-2242
Fax: 800-716-2242
E-mail: agoldstein@acf.dhhs.gov
http://ericps.crc.uiuc.edu/nccic/nccichome.html

CLINICAL SCHOOLS
American Association of Colleges for Teacher Education
One Dupont Circle, NW, Suite 610
Washington, DC 20036-1186
Phone: 202-293-2450
Toll Free: 800-822-9229
Fax: 202-457-8095
E-mail: iabdalha@inet.ed.gov
http://www.aacte.org/menu2.html

CONSUMER EDUCATION
National Institute for Consumer Education
207 Rackham Building
Eastern Michigan University
Ypsilanti, MI 48197
Phone: 313-487-2292
Fax: 313-487-7153
E-mail: Rosella.Bannister@emich.edu
http://www.emich.edu/public/coe/nice

ENTERPRENEURSHIP EDUCATION
Center for Enterpreneurial Leadership
Ewing Marion Kauffman Foundation
4900 Oak Street
Kansas City, MO 64112-2776
Phone: 816-932-1000
Toll Free: 800-423-5233
Fax: 310-825-9518
E-mail: celcee@ucla.edu
http://www.celcee.edu

ESL LITERACY EDUCATION
Center for Applied Linguistics
1118 22nd Street, NW
Washington, DC 20037-1214
Phone: 202-429-9292 ext. 200
Fax: 202-659-5641
E-mail: ncle@cal.org
http://www.cal.org/ncle

LAW-RELATED EDUCATION
Social Studies Development Center
Indiana University
2805 East Tenth Street, Suite 120
Bloomington, IN 47408
Phone: 812-855-3838
Toll Free: 800-266-3815
Fax: 812-855-0455
E-mail: ericso@indiana.edu
http://www.indiana.edu/~ssdc/lre.html

SERVICE LEARNING
University of Minnesota
College of Education and Human Development
1954 Bufford Avenue, Room R-290, VoTech Building
St. Paul, MN 55108
Phone: 612-625-6276
Toll Free: 800-808-SERV
Fax: 612-625-6277
E-mail: serv@maroon.tc.umn.edu
Gopher: gopher.nicsl.coled.umn.edu
http://www.nicsl.coled.umn.edu

TEST COLLECTION
Educational Testing Service
Princeton, NJ 08541
Phone: 609-734-5737
Fax: 609-683-7186
E-mail: mhalpern@ets.org
Gopher: gopher.cua.edu, Special Resources
http://www.cua.edu/www/eric_ae/testcol.html

U.S. – JAPAN STUDIES
Indiana University
Social Studies Development Center
2805 East 10th Street, Suite 120
Bloomington, IN 47408-2698
Phone: 812-855-3838
Toll Free: 800-266-3815
Fax: 812-855-04455
E-mail: japan@indiana.edu
http://www.indiana.edu/~japan**

Evaluation Form of a Proposal of a Research Study

1. Title (OK)

    1.1   ambiguous

    1.2   too long; make more concise

    1.3   awkward

    1.4   misleading

    1.5   not informative

2. Problem – Introduction (OK)

    2.1   background information missing

    2.2   too complex; needs delimitation

    2.3   significance of study not stated

    2.4   purpose stated irrelevant to study

    2.5   purpose too ambitious for the kind of research you are able to do

    2.6   problem incoherently presented

    2.7   theoretical framework for study missing

    2.8   relation of project to broader problems in the area missing

    2.9   statement of purpose missing

    2.10   state purpose more precisely

3. Related Research (OK)

    3.1   past research missing

    3.2   past research poorly integrated

    3.3   insufficient coverage of literature; important studies not cited

    3.4   research studies cited seem irrelevant to study

    3.5   topical organization missing

    3.6   lack of primary sources (for historical research)

    3.7   insufficient information presented regarding studies cited (e.g. purpose? design? findings? conclusions? limitations?)

    3.8   research studies merely listed, not critically evaluated (i.e. strengths and weaknesses not pointed out)

    3.9   relationship between related research and problem to be investigated not shown

3.10 references too dated; not enough recent, relevant studies are represented

3.11 summary of related research missing or poorly written

3.12 certain statements and/or studies not documented (or not correctly documented)

3.13 survey of past research acceptable at this time; however, pertinent studies should be incorporated for second draft

3.14 sources treated in too much detail for historical, documentary or construction type project

4. Operational Definitions (OK)

4.1 key terms and/or concepts not operationally defined

4.2 your definitions are not "operational" definitions

4.3 key terms and/or concepts inadequately defined

4.4 common words used in a special way not clarified

5. Assumptions – Delimitations (OK)

5.1 several assumptions implicit in study have not been recognized

5.2 delimitations not listed

5.3 several assumptions implicit in study not justifiable

5.4 delimitations confused with limitations

6. Hypothesis(es) or Question(s) (OK)

6.1 hypothesis (question) missing

6.2 hypothesis (question) not testable (cannot be answered) by your proposed study

6.3 hypothesis (question) poorly stated

6.4 hypothesis (question) unrelated to study

6.5 hypothesis (question) superficial

6.6 hypothesis (question) not related to theoretical framework developed in statement of problem

6.7 distinguish between research and statistical hypotheses

7. Method

a. Sample (OK)

7.1 description of population missing

7.2 sampling method missing

7.3 description of sample missing

7.4 description of sample incomplete

7.5 sample too small

b. Techniques – Instruments (OK)

7.6 techniques insufficiently described

7.7 rationale for use of instruments not given

7.8 rationale for use of proposed instruments unacceptable

7.9 sample questionnaire items missing

7.10 questionnaire items inappropriate

7.11 sample cover letter missing

7.12 sample cover letter poorly written

7.13 evidence regarding validity and/or reliability of instruments proposed missing

7.14 poor choice of instruments or techniques; consider using …

7.15 no provision made for pilot testing newly developed instruments

7.16 questionnaire (observation guide, interview guide, rating scale) poorly constructed

7.17 copy of instrument missing

c. Research Steps (OK)

7.18 indicate all research steps in the order in which they are to be carried out as well as time estimates for each step

7.19 research design inadequate because …

7.20 research design missing

7.21 research design unclear

7.22 several research steps missing

7.23 pilot study called for

d. Analysis of Data (OK)

7.24 principles of analysis and synthesis not indicated (for non-statistical projects)

7.25 tentative table of contents missing (for non-statistical projects)

7.26 statistical methods proposed to test each hypothesis (or to answer each question) missing

7.27 statistical analysis proposed is inappropriate

7.28 statistical analysis proposed stated incompletely

7.29 criterion of significance not stated

7.30 introduction missing (for non-statistical projects)

7.31 principles of criticism relating to authenticity, completeness and credibility not indicated (for non-statistical projects)

8. <u>Results, Conclusions, Generalizations, Implications, Limitations, Suggestions</u>

   a. <u>Results and Conclusions</u> (OK)

<u>8.1</u> results relating specifically to each hypothesis (or question) missing

<u>8.3</u> conclusions relating specifically to each hypothesis (or question) missing

<u>8.2</u> conclusions cannot be drawn from the study proposed

   b. <u>Generalizations</u> (OK)

<u>8.4</u> several possible generalizations missing

<u>8.5</u> stated generalizations not warranted

   c. <u>Implications</u> (OK)

<u>8.6</u> several possible implications missing

<u>8.7</u> incorrect implications have been stated

   d. <u>Limitations</u> (OK)

<u>8.8</u> several inherent limitations not stated

<u>8.9</u> incorrect limitations stated

   e. <u>Suggestions for Further Research</u> (OK)

<u>8.10</u> several possible suggestions for further research were not offered

<u>8.11</u> suggestions offered are not very meaningful

<u>8.12</u> Not enough suggestions for further research were offered

9. <u>References or Bibliography</u> (OK)

<u>9.1</u> all references missing

<u>9.3</u> reference pages incorrectly organized

<u>9.2</u> references incorrectly listed

<u>9.4</u> several references missing, e.g. _____

10. <u>Other Comments</u>

   a. <u>Writing Quality</u> (OK)

<u>10.1</u> too many errors in grammar, rhetoric, syntax, etc.

<u>10.2</u> too many spelling errors; proofread your paper prior to submission

10.3	immature writing style	10.5	writing is too opinionated and biased
10.4	writing tends to be awkward		

b. Organization (OK)

10.6   several recommendations with respect to format, style, and content were disregarded (e.g. disregard of outline format)

c. Action Taken on Proposal

10.7	proposal needs to be revised as indicated on draft and discussed in individual conference	10.8	proposal is acceptable with minor changes
		10.9	proposal is acceptable as is

d. Evaluation

10.10	very fine first draft	10.13	very disappointing
10.11	good beginning; now get to it	10.14	too skimpy; left too much out
10.12	scholarly and conscientious	10.15	look over a model proposal and follow it

APPENDIX E
Pedigree-Heritage Chart

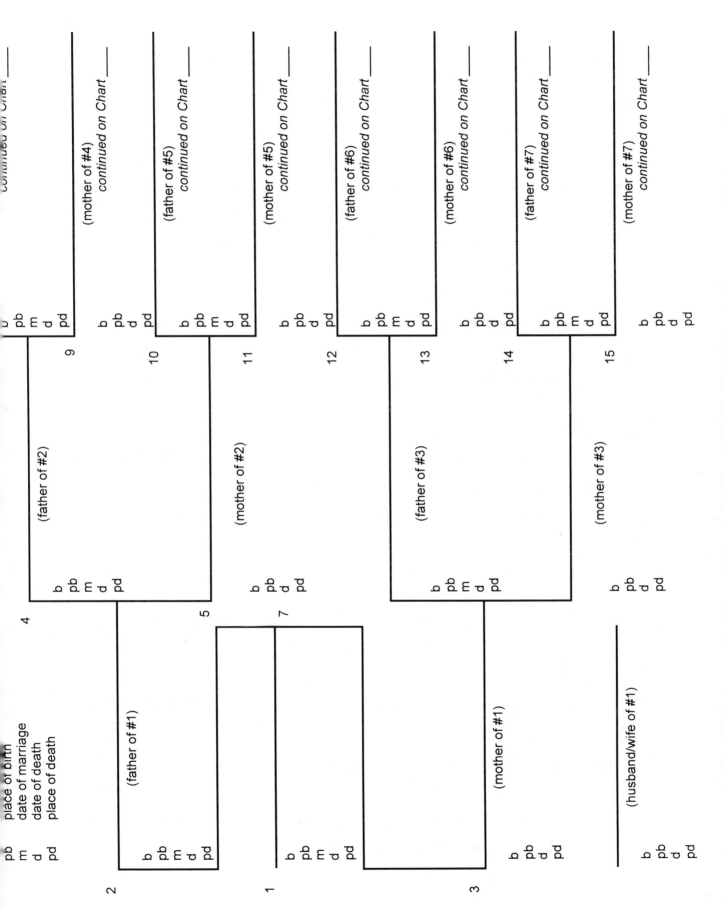

155

APPENDIX F

Procedure Section for a Non-Statistical Research Project

The product of this proposal is a death education curriculum for a nine-week mini-course offered at the 12th grade level in Midland Park High School. In order to fulfill this goal, it is necessary that research be done related to the rationale for this goal and the value that this program will have to students who participate in the course. Also, guidelines should be established to define the scope and design of the program. The author will then design, by synthesizing the related literature, an appropriate curriculum guide.

The steps required for this project and the anticipated time allotments are as follows:

Selection and approval of project	3 weeks
Location and evaluation of related literature	12 weeks
Analysis and synthesis of related literature	6 weeks
Writing the first draft	3 weeks
Criticism of and reworking the first draft	3 weeks
Typing and editing the final draft	3 weeks

Sources and Criticism

The sources for this project include books, ERIC reports, periodicals, pamphlets, and audio-visual materials. The periodicals and the ERIC reports were an invaluable source to curriculum guides, while the books presented a thorough review of the subject matter. (See the Review of the Literature for a detailed treatment).

External Criticism. It is not anticipated that the questions of authenticity or genuineness of the sources will raise problems. Therefore, the researcher does not feel required to submit the documents to the various stylistic and physical tests available to the historian. However, such questions as format clarity and completeness of the source may be helpful in judging its worth.

Internal Criticism. The problem of credibility or truthfulness may be a more difficult matter even in documentary based projects which are not fundamentally historical. The competency and bias of the author may bear investigating to help determine if the author is presenting a balanced and true picture.

Best and Kahn 1993) provide the beginning researcher with a practical list of questions to use as guides in establishing credibility. A sample of these questions follows:

1. Who is the author?
2. Is he or she competent and qualified to deal with this topic?
3. Did he or she have any personal motives for distorting the account?
4. Was the author subject to fear, pressure, or vanity?
5. How long after the event did he or she record the testimony?
6. Was he or she in agreement with competent witnesses?
7. Does the author make assumptions which are not logical?

Techniques of Analysis and Synthesis

The process of identifying, analyzing and synthesizing the information required for this project may proceed as follows:

1. Use the various preliminary sources – bibliographies, card catalogs, ERIC, etc. – to locate specific sources.
2. Compile annotated lists of sources, also indicating their physical location.
3. Judge material for appropriateness, completeness, and credibility.
4. Read sources selected, taking notes based on specific questions raised by this project.
5. As data are being gathered, attempt to conceptualize a logical outline for the finished product.
6. Arrange data topically and chronologically according to the format below.

<u>Tentative Table of Contents</u>

I.   General Information

    A.   Introduction and definition of death education
    B.   Philosophy
    C.   Rationale

II.   Objectives/Goals

    A. General and specific
    B. Teacher's goals – instructional objectives
    C. Student's goals – behavioral objectives

III.   Content

    A. Social
    B. Emotional
    C. Economic
    D. Other

IV.   Methods

    A. Practical, concrete
    B. Abstract
    C. Combination of practical and abstract
    D. Team teaching
    E. Teacher-student interaction
    F. Student-student interaction

V.   Materials

    A. Texts
    B. Novels
    C. Films
    D. Other audio-visual material
    E. Organizations
    F. Other

VI.   Suggested Activities

    A. Speakers
    B. Field trips
    C. Writing activities
    D. Other

VII.   Other Studies and Outcomes of Death Education

VIII.   Evaluation Techniques

IX.   Appendixes

    A.   Appendix I: bibliography of curriculum materials for teacher
    B.   Appendix II: bibliography of curriculum materials for student

APPENDIX G
Example of an Individual Case Study Outline

A. IDENTIFYING DATA

(name, address, phone number, date of birth, age, place of birth, gender, race, religion, national origin, marital status, occupation)

B. STATEMENT OF PROBLEM (as seen by client and referral agent)

C. FAMILY

(persons in home: father, mother, siblings, grandparents, other relatives, boarders, servants, etc.; home attitudes)

D. CULTURE

(culture group; cultural deviations and conflict – e.g. upward of downward mobility, generation gap, bilingual problems, etc.)

E. MEDICAL EXAMINATION AND HISTORY

(medical findings, physical development, illnesses and accidents, injuries, sexual development, etc.)

F. DEVELOPMENTAL HISTORY

(prenatal period, birth, early development, intellectual development, speech development, emotional development, social development)

G. EDUCATIONAL HISTORY

(school progress, educational achievement, school adjustment, educational aspirations and plans, etc.)

H. ECONOMIC HISTORY

(occupational history, vocational plans and ambitions, etc.)

I. LEGAL HISTORY

(delinquencies, court records – if any)

J. CLIENT'S LIFE

(lifestyle, interests, hobbies, recreational pursuits, fantasy life, friends, etc.)

APPENDIX H

Example of a Community Case Study Outline

(An Evaluation of the Chicago Community Action Program)

Chapter

1   The Community Action Program

        History and Goals of Community Action Programs
        History and Goals of the Chicago Community Action Program
        Theoretical Framework of the Study
        Hypotheses of the Study

2   Operational Definitions

        Review of Evaluative Research
        Concepts and Indicators of Social Control and Influence
        Definitions of Indicators

3   The Structure and Functioning of the Chicago Community Action Program

        Council Against Poverty
        Community Development Agency
        Poverty Areas in Chicago
        Structure of the Shore Community Program
        Delegate Agencies in the Shore Area

4   Methods and Sampling

        Techniques of Participant Observation
        Techniques of Interviewing
        Development of Categories for Sample
        Sample Group I: Participants
        Sample Group II: Non-participants
        Sample Group III: The Youths
        Evaluation of Methods Used

5   Findings of Observational Data

        Neighborhood Groups
        Program Personnel
        Neighborhood Clients
        Conclusion: Summary in Terms of Indicators

6   Findings of Interview Data

        Neighborhood Groups
        Program Personnel
        Neighborhood Clients
        Conclusions

Chapter

APPENDIX I

Illustrative Outline of a Historical Research Project

(Major Factors in the Growth and Development
of Science Education in the U.S.: 1893-1997)

Chapter

1   Introduction

          Statement of the Problem
          Background of the Study
          Significance of the Study
          Assumptions and Delimitations of the Study
          Definition of Terms
          Related Literature
          Procedures

2   Some Societal Changes That Have Affected the Science Education Curriculum

3   Science Education in the Curriculum: 1893-1915

4   Science Education in the Curriculum: 1916-1930

5   Science Education in the Curriculum: 1931-1946

6   Science Education in the Curriculum: 1947-1969

7   Science Education in the Curriculum: 1970-1997

8   Summary and Conclusions

          The Period 1893-1915

          The Period 1916-1930

          The Period 1931-1946

          The Period 1947-1969

          The Period 1970-1997

      Appendix

      Bibliography

APPENDIX J

Illustrative Outline of a Bibliographical Research Project

(Sexism and Reading: An Analysis and Synthesis
of the Empirical Studies and Expert Opinion)

Chapter

1   Introduction

          Statement of Problem and Objectives
          Background and Significance of the Study
          Assumptions and Delimitations of the Study
          Definition of Terms
          Related Literature
          Procedures

2   Types of Materials Chosen by Researchers for Study

3   Methods of Analysis Used by Researchers

4   Purposes of Studying Stereotyping

5   Major Findings of Studies of Sexism in Reading Materials

6   Criticisms of Studies of Sexism in Reading Materials

7   Summary and Recommendations for Further Studies

      Appendix

      Bibliography

APPENDIX K

Illustrative Outline of a Documentary Research Project

(Career Development Theories in Vocational Guidance:

The Current Major Schools of Thought)

Chapter

1   Introduction

          Problem and Objectives
          Background of the Study
          Significance of the Study
          Assumptions and Delimitations
          Definitions
          Related Literature
          Procedures

2   Ginzberg's Developmental Theory

3   Roe's Need Theory

4   Super's Developmental, Self-Concept Theory

5   Holland's Career Typology Theory

6   Tiedeman's Developmental, Decision-making Theory

7   Trait and Factor Theory

8   Other Decision-Making Theories

9   Some Conclusions About Present Theory Construction

10   Trends for the Future of Theory Construction

      Appendix

      Bibliography

APPENDIX L

Illustrative Outline of a Construction Research Project

(The Development of a Twelfth Grade Nine-Week Mini-Course on Death)

Chapter

1   Introduction

> Statement of Problem and Objectives
> Background and Significance of the Study
> Assumptions and Delimitations
> Definitions of Terms
> Related Literature
> Procedures

2   Introduction to Death Education

> Definitions
> Philosophy
> Rationale

3   Goals and Objectives of Death Education

> General Educational Goals
> General Teacher Goals
> Specific Teacher Goals: Instructional Objectives
> General Student Goals
> Specific Student Goals: Behavioral Objectives

4   Subject Matter Content

> Social
> Emotional
> Economic
> Other

5   Methods and Techniques

> Teacher Centered: Lecture, Demonstration, etc.
> Student Centered: Problem-solving, etc.
> Team Teaching
> Other

6   Materials for Teachers and Students

> Books, Journals, and Pamphlets
> Films and Other Audio-Visual Aids
> Organizations and Community Resources
> Other

Chapter

7   Suggested Activities

                 Writing and Project Activities
                 Field Trips
                 Speakers
                 Other

8   Examples of Model Lesson Plans

9   Evaluation Techniques

10   Appendixes
                 Teacher Resources
                 Student Resources

APPENDIX M
Protocol Format

Name of researcher: Page_____of_____

Date of observation:

Subject of observation:

Site of observation:

Protocol number:

1

2

3

4

5

6

7

8

9

10

11

12

13

14

15

16

17

18

19

20

(_Formal_ data collection via this technique requires the writing of a continuous and complete observation. An _informal_ approach is more sporadic and anecdotal, but also requires the researcher's complete attention. The _recollective_ record is made entirely from memory.)

GLOSSARY

Abstract. A very succinct version of a research report consisting of the problem statement along with brief treatments of the procedures, findings and implications. Not same as a summary.

Achievement Test. An assessment device which measures the extent to which a person has acquired or mastered certain subject matter content or skills.

Action Research. Research that leads to action. Applying research techniques to problems of local concern. Less rigorous than basic or applied research.

Affective Domain. Those behaviors dealing with changes in a person's attitudes, feelings, values, personality and emotions.

Analysis of Covariance. Used when compared groups are initially unequal. A test of significance which statistically adjusts the two groups to make them equivalent. It does not replace random assignment.

Analysis of Variance (ANOVA). Used when a number of groups are to be compared. A test of statistical significance which, when comparing differences among means, produces an F-ratio, which expresses the ratio of variations caused by the treatment to variations caused by error.

Appendix. A section added to a book or report which contains details to supplement the text and, if placed in with the text, would tend to disrupt the narrative.

Applied Research. Applying research techniques to practical problems of some general concern. Goes beyond action research in both scope and rigor. Can involve sophisticated procedures and aims to apply the research results to the larger population.

Aptitude Test. An assessment device designed to predict future performance on some activity. Aptitudes are those characteristics that indicate the ability to learn or develop a proficiency, given the appropriate education and conditions.

Association Study. A project which attempts to determine if there is a statistical relationship (its strength and direction) between two variables. Examples are correlational and prediction studies.

Basic Research. Applying research techniques to conceptual or theoretical problems. There need be no practical application in mind; rather, the aim is to discover new knowledge and build new theory as an end in themselves.

Bivariate. The study of two variables at once.

Closed-End Question. An item that presents a choice of prepared answers. The answer must be selected.

Cluster Sample. A variation of random sampling where the unit selected is a group of "cluster" rather than a single subject. The units or groups are then selected randomly. This technique may save time and money, but is not true random sampling.

Cognitive Domain. Those behaviors dealing with changes in a person's learning in the areas of knowledge, concept building, understanding principles, solving problems, etc.

Concurrent Validity. The degree to which one assessment technique agrees with or correlates with another assessment technique that is believed to measure the same thing.

Construct Validity. The degree to which the assessment technique is actually measuring the characteristics (construct) it claims to measure.

Content Validity. The degree to which the assessment technique actually measures a representative sample or a balanced sample of the objectives that it is supposed to measure.

Control Group. The group that does not receive the treatment in an experiment and is used to provide a standard against which the experimental group is compared.

Correlation Coefficient. A statistical index used to express the strength and direction of a relationship between variables. It is usually written as a decimal ranging from –1.00 to +1.00.

Correlation Study. Comparison of two or more variables to determine strength and direction of relationship. A high correlation indicates they are strongly related. A low correlation indicates little or no relationship; no cause and effect relationship is implied.

Criterion Referenced Test. A test in which the subject's score is compared to some predetermined standard (the criterion) rather than to other subjects who took the test (the norm).

Critical-incident-technique. A method of studying people by observing selected samples of their behavior and drawing conclusions about their general behavior.

Demographic Data. Identification and background information obtained on the subjects such as age, gender, grade, social class, etc.

Dependent Variable. The variable that is changed by or "depends" on the treatment for its value. Sometimes referred to as the outcome or criterion variable. The measurement or observation that takes place to determine if the treatment had the expected effect.

Descriptive Research. Research studies that seek to explain and predict. Existing conditions and variables are used with no manipulation. Direct cause and effect relationships cannot be obtained.

Descriptive Statistics. Procedures and formulas for collecting, organizing, analyzing, interpreting and presenting numerical data obtained on some population or sample. Calculating measures of central tendency, variability, relative position and relationship.

Differential Selection. A threat to internal validity which is caused by the process through which individuals are placed into groups. A bias may result if the researcher cannot use randomization to equate the groups.

Empirical Data. Verifiable information derived form careful observation and measurement.

Equivalent Forms Reliability. The degree to which two forms of the same test are similar. It is estimated statistically by computing a correlation coefficient obtained by comparing the same group on two forms of the same test.

Ethnographic Research. A method to carry out qualitative observational research in naturally occurring situations.

Experimental Mortality. A threat to internal validity when subjects, for one reason or another, do not complete the study (e.g. death, illness, leave town or decide not to participate).

Experimental Research. Research which attempts to determine cause and effect through maximum control of the variables which interfere with the treatment being given to one group (experimental group) while withholding it from another group (the control group).

Experimental Variable. The treatment or stimulus administered to the experimental group between pretest and posttest.

External Criticism. Attempts to ascertain the genuineness and authenticity of a source.

External Validity. The degree to which the results of research project can be generalized beyond the subjects and setting of the study.

Extraneous Variable. Any variable, not manipulated by the experimenter, which may affect the outcome of an experiment and thus should be controlled.

Face Validity. The degree to which the person who is taking a test or some other assessment device perceives it to be measuring the construct it is said to measure.

Factorial Design. A research design which allows the experimenter to deal systematically with several independent variables. Such a design provides results for the effects of each separate independent variable as well as the interactions of these variables on the dependent variable.

Frequency Distribution. A tabulation of scores of a group of individuals to show the frequency of each score, or those within the range of each interval.

Generalizability. The degree to which research findings are applicable to a wider group than was actually studied. Random selection of subjects used in the research is required to make inferences to the population form which they come.

Hawthorne Effect. The tendency of people to respond positively to being singled out for study.

Heterogeneity. Variety in a group. A group with a wide range of scores.

History. Extraneous events other than the experimental variable, occurring during the experiment, that may affect the results of the study.

Homogeneity. Uniformity in a group. A group with a narrow range of scores.

Hypothesis, Null. A statistical hypothesis, also called the no-difference hypothesis. A statement that indicates that the differences found between variables in an experimental design are due to chance variation and not true differences caused by the treatment. Used to assess the statistical significance of the results.

Hypothesis, Research. A statement of relation between two more variables that is being tested. It represents the expectations of the researcher.

Independent Variable. The variable that is manipulated in experimental research to cause change in the dependent variable. Also called the experimental and treatment variable.

Instrumentation. One of the extraneous variables that threatens the internal validity of an experimental design; when the measuring instrument loses its effectiveness. For example, springs in a scale may lose some of their tension, or long questionnaires may cause fatigue or loss of interest.

Interaction. The effect of two or more independent variables on a dependent variable. This effect is different from the separate of main effects of each independent variable. Interaction can be studied in factorial designs.

Internal Criticism. Attempts to ascertain the truthfulness and credibility of the source (e.g. possible bias of the author).

Internal Validity. The degree to which the results of the experiment can be said to be caused solely by the treatment variable rather than one of the various extraneous variables.

Interval Data. A level of measurement in which there are equal intervals between units on the scale. The numerical data at this level are continuous, thus allowing a full range of mathematical operations.

Intervening Variable. Also known as the organismic variable. It resides within the organism (e.g. anxiety, fatigue, motivation).

Interview Schedule. A structured guide comprised of a series of questions or general topics that are asked and then answers filled in by the interviewer.

Interviewer Effect. Changes in a subject's behavior because she or he is reacting to the presence of the interviewer.

Justification for the Study. A section in the introduction of the research proposal which delineates the reasons for doing the study. Research literature as well as aspects of the real life situation may be cited as support.

Kuder – Richardson Reliability Coefficient. A statistical procedure for estimating the internal consistency of a test.

Level of Significance. The probability of rejecting the null hypothesis when it is true. Also known as the alpha level.

Levels of Measurement. A hierarchy of four levels of measurement scales arranged from simple to complex according to the properties of each level. The quantitative value and thus the statistical power of the data increase at each level: nominal, ordinal, interval and ratio.

Matching. Attempting to equate groups by selecting two groups of subjects who are similar in one or more characteristics, forming two parallel or matched groups.

Maturation. A threat to internal validity caused by changes in time rather than as a result of the treatment that occurred while time was passing.

Mean. A measure of central tendency or typicality. Also called the arithmetic average. It is obtained by dividing the sum of a distribution set of scores by the number of scores.

Median. A measure of central tendency that represents the midpoint of a distribution of scores. It is not affected by extreme scores, as is the mean.

Meta-analysis. A research procedure that uses statistical techniques to combine the results of different research studies.

Mode. A measure of central tendency that is the score which occurs most frequently in the distribution. The simplest and crudest measure of central tendency.

Multiple Correlation. Correlation of more than two variables at the same time.

Multivariate Analysis. The simultaneous analysis of three or more variables for the purpose of prediction or to control for selected factors.

Negative Correlation. Two variables varying in opposite directions; as the scores of one increase, the scores of the other decrease.

Nominal Data. The lowest level of measurement, where data can only be assigned to categories; numerals function only to identify and classify.

Nonparametric Test. A statistical test of significance used to analyze categorical data or higher level data treated as categorical that are not normally distributed.

Norm Referenced Test. A test in which the subject's score is compared to the scores of others who took the test (the norm) rather than to some predetermined criterion.

Normal Distribution. A symmetrical frequency distribution where most of the scores fall near the mean but fewer and fewer scores fall near the extremes of the distribution. The normal distribution is characteristic of most psychological and physical data and is used as a model for many scoring systems and statistical analyses. A bell-shaped curve is formed with the mean, median and mode at the same point on the curve.

One-Tailed Test. A test of statistical significance used when the research hypothesis predicts a direction of the results. In a one-tailed test, the area of rejection in only one end of the sampling distribution is used.

Open-Ended Question. An item that does not suggest any choice of answers and the respondent is free to give his/her own answer.

Operational Definition. A definition of a variable that assigns meaning to it by specifying the observable behaviors or measures that will represent the variable. This is a crucial step in making research objective and verifiable.

Ordinal Data. A level of measurement which permits data to be classified and ranked, but which does not allow numbers to represent exact scores; there is not fixed value between ranks.

Parameter. The value of a statistical characteristic for total population.

Parametric Test. A statistical test used to determine if inferences made from sample data to the population are significant. This type of test assumes interval or ratio level data and that one or more of the variables is (are) normally distributed.

Percentile. A score in a distribution below which fall the percentage of cases indicated by the percentile.

Percentile Rank. The percentage of scores in a norm group that are equal to or lower than a given score on a test.

Population. The total number of people of concern to the researcher from which the sample is drawn.

Positive Correlation. Two or more variables changing in the same direction. That is, as one increases, the other increases as well.

Practical Significance. The degree to which research results are suitable or can be adapted to real world conditions and problems. Data may be statistically but not practically significant.

Plagiarism. Using someone else's words, ideas or illustrations without giving him or her credit.

Posttest. The test given after the experimental group has received the treatment.

Prediction Study. Research which attempts to determine whether a known correlation between two variables in one situation holds true in a separate but similar situation. Data on one of the variables are used to estimate the values of a second variable.

Predictive Validity. The degree to which an assessment technique predicts the respondent's performance on some future task.

Pretest. The test given before the experimental group has received the treatment.

Pretesting. A threat to internal and external validity that occurs when taking the pretest benefits the respondent in such a way that he or she can obtain higher scores on the posttest.

Primary Sources. The direct record or description of an occurrence by an individual who actually witnessed or observed the event.

Probability. The likelihood of something happening by chance.

Qualitative Research. A study that relies upon data collected via open-ended narrative and observation. It is based on detailed descriptions of events, people and excerpts from various letters, records and other documents. Thus it is basically verbal in database and analysis.

Quantitative Research. A study that relies upon variables that can be measured. The data can then be collected, organized and interpreted via statistical techniques.

Quasi-Experiment. An experiment characterized by lack of control over subjects.

Quota Sampling. A non-random procedure where the population is stratified and a percentage of each stratum is selected.

Random Assignment. Selecting subjects for groups in such a way that all subjects have an equal chance of being assigned to any of the groups.

Random Sample. Each subject has an equal chance of being chosen, and the selection of any one subject has no effect on the selection of any other. Also known as random selection.

Random Selection. (See Random Sample).

Range. The simplest measure of variability expressed as the difference between the highest and lowest score in the distribution.

Rating Scale. An assessment device which contains a series of number points, descriptive statements or behavioral categories that an observer uses to indicate the degree of a characteristic a person possesses.

Ration Data. The most refined level of measurement, as it has all the properties of the nominal, ordinal and interval levels plus a true zero point. Thus, a full range of statistical operations can be done.

Reactive Measure. An assessment device that sensitizes respondents to certain events. It can be a source of bias which may change the subject's responses.

Reliability. The degree to which an assessment device is consistent or dependable.

Reliability Coefficient. A numerical indicator of the degree of consistency shown by a measuring instrument.

Replication Study. Repetition of a research project, usually with comparable subjects and at a different time. Even though procedures are the same, it normally requires a justification based on prior weakness in the original study or new needs emanating from the present situation.

Research Problem. A succinct description of the research topic and techniques so that a clear-cut purpose of the research project is evident. "Problem" may be used interchangeably with "purpose of the study."

Respondent. A person who responds to a research instrument.

Response Set. A style of responding to a research instrument that emanates from the subject's values, biases or background.

Sample. A subgroup drawn form a population.

Sampling Bias. The degree to which the sample does not reflect the characteristics of the population.

Sampling Distribution. A frequency distribution that consists of the means obtained from drawing repeated random samples of a fixed size from the same population.

Sampling Error. The difference between a statistic and the corresponding parameter.

Scientific Method. A procedure for generating empirical data, generally characterized by tentativeness, openness, rigorous reasoning and verifiability.

Secondary Sources. The indirect record or description of an occurrence by an individual who did not witness or observe the event.

Stability. The degree to which an instrument produces similar results with repeated administrations. Can be estimated statistically by a test-retest reliability coefficient.

Standard Deviation. A measure of the dispersion or heterogeneity of a set of scores around the mean of the set. It can be thought of as the square root of the variance. (See Variance.)

Standard Error of the Mean. The standard deviation of a sampling distribution of means. The statistical bridge that connects the sample and the population and forms one of the bases of inferential statistics.

Standard Score. A type of converted score that denotes how many standard deviation units the raw score deviates from the mean; examples are z scores and T scores.

Standardized Assessment Device. An instrument having specified content, prescribed procedures for scoring and administration, and normative data for interpreting scores.

Statistic. The value of a statistical characteristic for a sample.

Statistical Regression. The threat to internal validity that results from the tendency of the extreme scores of groups to move toward the mean on subsequent tests.

Statistical Significance. The statistical probability that an observed result could have happened by chance. Results are considered statistically significant when the chances are very low [1 out of 100 (.01) or 5 out of 100 (.05)] that they happened by chance.

Statistical Random Sampling. A variation of random sampling in which subjects in the population are subdivided in strata according to specific characteristics prior to their selection. A predetermined number of subjects per strata are then selected randomly to ensure a proper representation of each strata in the population.

Structured Item. (See Closed-End Question.)

Subject. The person who participates in a research study. Subjects may be volunteers, people selected on convenience, or people chosen by statistically sound methods.

Systematic Sampling. A sample selected form a list at fixed intervals, the first selection having been made at random.

Table of Random Numbers. A table used to select subjects randomly and made up of a list of numbers compiled by a random process.

Treatment. Procedures administered to subjects in an experiment to discover if an effect is produced in the dependent variable. Also called the independent or experimental variable.

True Experimental Design. A research plan that attempts to control the contaminating variables through random selection and assignment of subjects. This is the ultimate design in research aimed at determining causality.

True Score. The score a person would obtain on a perfectly reliable test; the score obtained on a test with an infinite number of items or equivalent forms; a theoretical score never attainable in the real world.

t-Test. A statistical procedure to determine significant differences between sample means and the significance of correlation coefficients.

Type I Error. Rejecting the null hypothesis when it is really true; that is, assuming statistical significance that is not there.

Type II Error. Accepting the null hypothesis when it is really false; that is, mistakenly assuming lack of statistical significance.

Univariate. Pertaining to a single variable.

Unobtrusive Measurement. A way of collecting data without coming in contact with the subject, who is thus not likely to "react" to this process.

Validity. The degree to which a procedure or device does what it claims to do. Content, concurrent, predictive and construct validity all deal with how well an assessment device does what it is supposed to do. The two types of experimental validity (internal and external validity) ask the question: Did the experimental treatment really produce the results obtained?

Variable. A characteristic, condition or trait that can take on different values.

Variance. A measure of dispersion or heterogeneity of a set of scores around the mean of the set. It takes into account every score and its size and distance form the mean of its set. It is obtained by summing the squared deviations form the mean and dividing this sum by the number of scores. The square root of this result is called the standard deviation.

Within-Groups Variance. The variation of scores from all groups in a study around the mean of the scores. It is assumed that the variance reflects the variation in the larger population from which the subjects were drawn. This variation is due to sampling error and also called chance variation.

BIBLIOGRAPHY

Alkin, M.C. (Ed.) (1992). <u>Encyclopedia of educational research</u>. New York: Macmillan.

American Psychological Association (1982). <u>Ethical principles in the conduct of research with human participants</u>. Washington, D.C.:Author.

American Psychological Association (1988). <u>Standards for educational and psychological testing</u>. Washington, D.C.: Author.

American Psychological Association (1994). <u>Publication manual</u> (4th ed.).Washington, D.C.: Author.

Anastasi, A. and Urbina, S. (1997). <u>Psychological testing</u> 7th ed.) Engelwood Cliffs, NJ: Prentice Hall.

Anderson, J.F. (1986). <u>Questionnaire design and use</u>. (2nd. ed.). Metuchen, N.J.: Scarecrow Press.

Arbib, M.A. (1984). <u>Computers and the cybernetic society</u> (2nd ed.) New York: Academic Press.

Barzun, J. and Graff, H.P. (1992). <u>The modern researcher</u> (5th ed.). San Diego, Ca.: Harcourt Brace College Publishers.

Beere, C.A. (1990). <u>Gender roles: A handbook of tests and measures</u>. San Francisco: Greenwood.

Beere, C.A. (1990). <u>Sex and gender issues: A handbook of tests and measures</u>. San Francisco: Greenwood.

Berry, D.M. (1990) <u>Bibliographic guide to educational research</u> (3rd ed.) Metuchen, N.J.: Scarecrow Press.

Best, J.W. and Kahn, J.V. (1993). <u>Research in education</u> (7th ed.). Boston, MA: Allyn – Bacon.

Bonney, M.E. (1960) Sociometric methods. In C.W. Harris (Ed.) <u>Encyclopedia of educational research</u> (3rd ed.) New York: Macmillan.

Bruning, J.L. and Kintz, B.L. (1997). <u>Computational handbook of statistics</u> (4th ed.). Reading, MA: Addison Wesley Longman.

Byham, W.C. and Bobin, D. (Eds.) (1973) <u>Alternatives to paper and pencil testing</u>. Pittsburgh: Graduate School of Business, University of Pittsburgh.

Campbell, D.T. and Stanley, J.C. (1966). <u>Experimental and quasi-experimental designs for research</u>. Boston: Houghton – Mifflin.

Campbell, W.G. et al. (1990). <u>Form and style: theses, reports, term papers</u> (8th ed.). Boston: Houghton – Mifflin.

Cohen, J. (1988). <u>Statistical power analysis</u> (2nd ed.) New York: Academic Press.

Conoley, J.C. and Impara, James C. (Eds.) (1995). <u>The twelfth mental measurements yearbook</u>. Lincoln, NE: Buros Institute of Mental Measurements

Cronbach, L.J. (1990). <u>Essentials of psychological testing</u> (5th ed.). Reading, MA: Addison Wesley Educational Publishers, Inc.

Davidson, H.H. and Lang, G. (1990). Children's perception of their teacher's feelings toward them related to self-perceptions, school achievement, and behavior. <u>Journal of Experimental Education, 29</u>, 107-118.

Dewey, J. (1991). <u>How we think</u>. New York: Prometheus Books.

Downie, N.M. and Heath, R.W. (1983) <u>Basic statistical methods</u> (5th ed.). New York: Harper and Row.

Ferguson, G.A. (1989). <u>Statistical analysis in psychology and education</u> (6th ed.). New York: McGraw-Hill.

Flanagan, J.C. (1954). The critical-incident technique. <u>Psychological Bulletin</u>, 51, 327-358.

Forcese, D.P. and Richter, S. (1973). <u>Social research methods</u>. Englewood Cliffs, N.J.: Prentice-Hall.

Fredman, N. and Sherman, R. (1987). <u>Handbook of measurements for marriage and family therapy</u>. New York: Brunner/Mazel.

Gall, Meredith D., Borg, Walter, and Gall, Joyce P. (1996). <u>Educational research: an introduction</u> (6th ed.). New York: Longman.

Glass, G.V. McGaw, B. and Smith, M.L. (1981). <u>Meta-analysis in social research</u>. Newbury Park; CA: Sage.

Goldman, B.A. et al. (1974-1995). <u>Directory of unpublished experimental mental measures</u>. Volumes I-VI.

Gottschalk, L.M. (1969). <u>Understanding history</u>. New York: Alfred A. Knopf.

Gottschalk, L.M. et al. (1945). <u>The use of personal documents in history, anthropology and sociology</u> (Bulletin No. 53) New York: Social Science Research Council.

Grahm, N. (1989). <u>The mind tool: computers and their impact on society (with BASIC appendix)</u> (5th ed.). New York: West.

Gronlund, N.E. and Linn, R.L. (1989). <u>Measurement and evaluation in teaching</u>: (6th ed.). New York: Macmillan.

Guilford, J.P. and Fruchter, B. (1978). <u>Fundamental statistics in psychology and education</u> (6th ed.). New York: McGraw-Hill.

Jaeger, R. M. (1984). <u>Sampling in education and the social sciences</u>, New York: Longman.

Johnson, O.G. and Bommarito, J.W. (1971). <u>Tests and measurements in child development: handbook II</u>. San Francisco: Jossey-Bass.

Johnson, O.G. (1976). <u>Tests and measurements in child development: handbook II</u> (2 vols.). San Francisco: Jossey-Bass.

Kerlinger, F.N. (1986). <u>Foundations of behavioral research</u> (3rd ed.). San Diego, CA: Harcourt Brace College Publishers.

Keyser, D.J. and Sweetland, R.C. (Eds.) (1994). <u>Test critiques</u> (Volumes I – X). Austin, Texas: Pro-Ed.

Koenker, R.H. (1971). <u>Simplified statistics for students in education and psychology</u>. Totowa, N.J.: Littlefield, Adams.

Kraemer, H.C. and Thiemann, S. (1987). <u>How many subjects? Statistical power analysis in research</u>. Newbury Park, CA: Sage.

Lang, G. (1997). <u>A practical guide to statistics for research and measurement</u>. Upper Montclair, NJ: Montclair State University.

LeCompte, M.D. and Preissle, J. (1993). <u>Ethnography and qualitative design in educational research</u> (2nd ed.). Orlando, FL: Academic Press.

Linn, R.L. (Ed.) (1989). <u>Educational measurement</u> (3rd ed.) New York: Macmillan.

McWilliams, P.A. (1990). <u>The personal computer book</u>. Los Angeles, CA: Prelude Press.

Marchall, C. and Rossman, G.R. (1989). <u>Designing qualitative research</u>. Newbury Park, CA: Sage.

Medley, D.M. and Mitzel, H. (1963). Measuring classroom behavior by systematic observation. In N.L. Gage (Ed.) <u>Handbook of research on teaching</u>. Chicago: Rand McNally.

Murphy, Linda U., Conoley, Jane C., and Impara, James C. (Eds.) (1994). <u>Tests in print IV</u>. Lincoln, NE: Buros Institute of Mental Measurements, The University of Nebraska.

Patton, M.Q. (1990). <u>Qualitative evaluation research methods</u> (2nd ed.) Newbury Park, CA: Sage.

Robinson, J.P. and Shaver, P.R. (1973). <u>Measures of social psychological attitudes</u> (rev. ed). Ann Arbor, MI: Institute for Social Research, University of Michigan.

Rosenthal, R. (1991). <u>Meta-analytic procedures for social research</u>. Newbury Park, CA: Sage.

Sax, G. (1997). <u>Principles of educational measurement and evaluation</u> (4th ed.). Belmont, CA: Wadsworth.

Siegel, S. and Castellan, N.J. (1988). <u>Non-parametric statistics</u> (2nd ed.) New York: McGraw-Hill.

Snider, J.G. and Osgood, C.E. (Eds.) (1969). <u>Semantic differential technique: A sourcebook</u>. Chicago, ILL: Aldine.

Stewart, C.J., and Cash, W.B. (1996). <u>Interviewing: principles and practices</u>. (8th ed.). Madison, WI: Brown and Benchmark.

Strauss, A. and Corbin, J. (1990) <u>Basics of qualitative research: Grounded theory procedures and techniques</u>. Newbury Park, CA: Sage.

Strunk, W. Jr. and White, E.B. (1995). <u>The elements of style</u>. Des Moines, IA: Allyn and Bacon, Inc.

Sudman, S. and Brodman, N.M. (1982). <u>Asking questions</u>. San Francisco: Jossey – Bass.

Sweetland, R.C. and Keyser, D,J. (Eds.) (1991). <u>Tests: A comprehensive reference for assessments in psychology, education and business</u> (3rd ed.) Austin, Texas: Pro-Ed.

Tuckman, B.W. (1994). <u>Conducting educational research</u> (4th ed.). New York: Harcourt Brace Jovanovich.

U.S. Office of Strategic Services (1948). <u>Assessment of men</u>. New York: Rinehart.

Watts, J.F. and Davis, A.F. (1983). <u>Generations: Your family in modern American history</u> (3rd ed.) New York: Knopf.

Winer, B.J. (1991). <u>Statistical principles in experimental design</u> (3rd ed.). New York: The McGraw Hill Company.

Wolf, F.M. (1986) <u>Meta-analysis: Quantitative methods for research synthesis</u>. Newbury Park, CA: Sage.

INDEX